I Can Draw...
Creepy Crawlies

Artwork by Terry Longhurst
Text by Amanda O'Neill

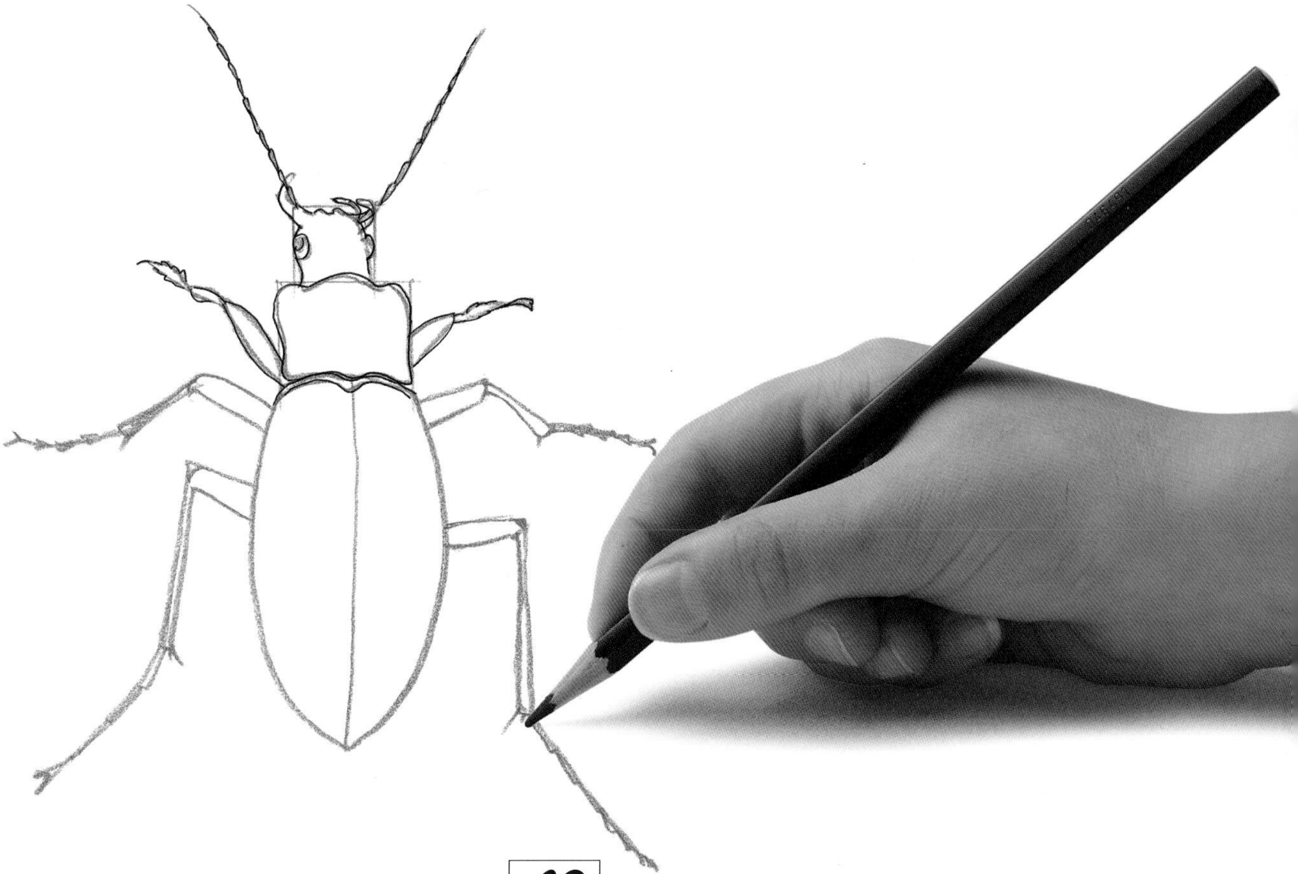

p

This is a Parragon Book
This edition published in 2003

Parragon
Queen Street House
4 Queen Street
Bath BA1 1HE, UK

Designed, packaged, and produced by
Touchstone

Hardback: ISBN 1-40540-350-0
Paperback: ISBN 1-40540-034-X

Artwork by Terry Longhurst
Text by Amanda O'Neill
Edited by Philip de Ste. Croix

Printed in Dubai,U.A.E

About this book

Everybody can enjoy drawing, but sometimes it's hard to know where to begin. The subject you want to draw can look very complicated. This book shows you how to start, by breaking down your subject into a series of simple shapes.

The tools you need are very simple. The basic requirements are paper and pencils. Very thin paper wears through if you have to rub out a line, so choose paper that is thick enough to work on. Pencils come with different leads, from very hard to very soft. Very hard pencils give a clean, thin line which is best for finishing drawings. Very soft ones give a thicker, darker line. You will probably find a medium pencil most useful.

If you want to colour in your drawing, you have the choice of paints, coloured inks, or felt-tip pens. Fine felt-tips are useful for drawing outlines, thick felt-tips are better for colouring in.

The most important tool you have is your own eyes. The mistake many people make is to draw what they think something looks like, instead of really looking at it carefully first. Half the secret of making your drawing look good is getting the proportions right. Study your subject before you start, and break it down in your mind into sections. Check how much bigger, or longer, or shorter, one part is than another. Notice where one part joins another, and at what angle. See where there are flowing curves, and where there are straight lines.

The step-by-step drawings in this book show you exactly how to do this. Each subject is broken down into easy stages, so you can build up your drawing one piece at a time. Look carefully at each shape before - and after - you draw it. If you find you have drawn it the wrong size or in the wrong place, correct it before you go on. Then the next shape will fit into place, and piece-by-piece you can build up a fantastic picture.

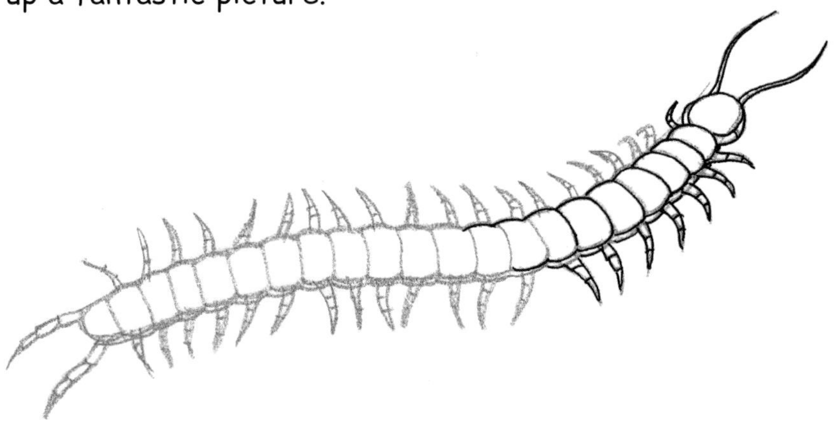

Dragonfly

Dragonflies are found all over the world – more than 2500 different kinds of them. In summer they can be seen flashing over ponds and rivers. These are their hunting grounds, where they catch smaller flying insects. Their swift, graceful flight and brilliant colours are eye-catching.

Starting couldn't be simpler – just draw a long rectangle. The outspread wings will fit into this shape.

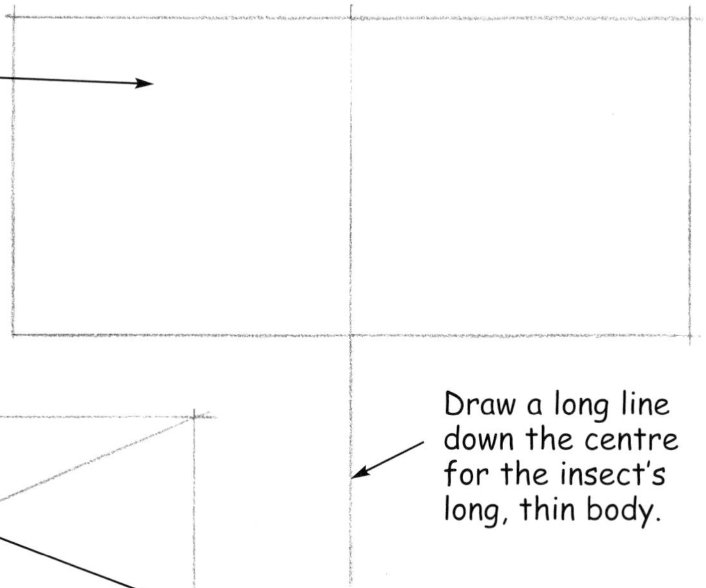

Draw a long line down the centre for the insect's long, thin body.

These slanting lines mark the outside edges of the two pairs of wings.

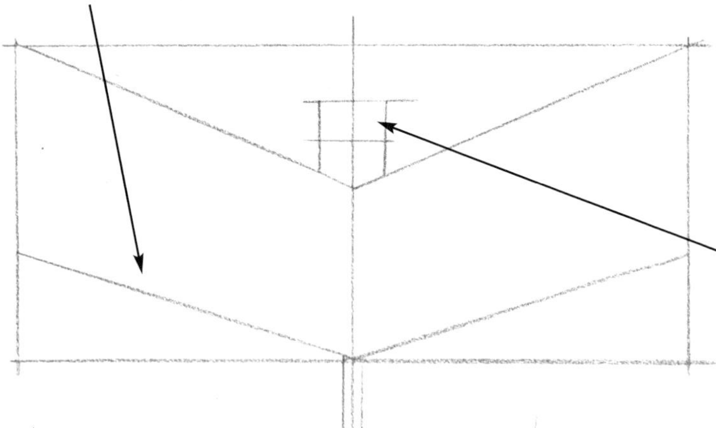

Draw in guidelines for the insect's head and upper body. The head is quite large.

The long, thin body sticks out well beyond the wings. It is shaped rather like a blunt needle – in fact, people used to call dragonflies 'the devil's darning needles'.

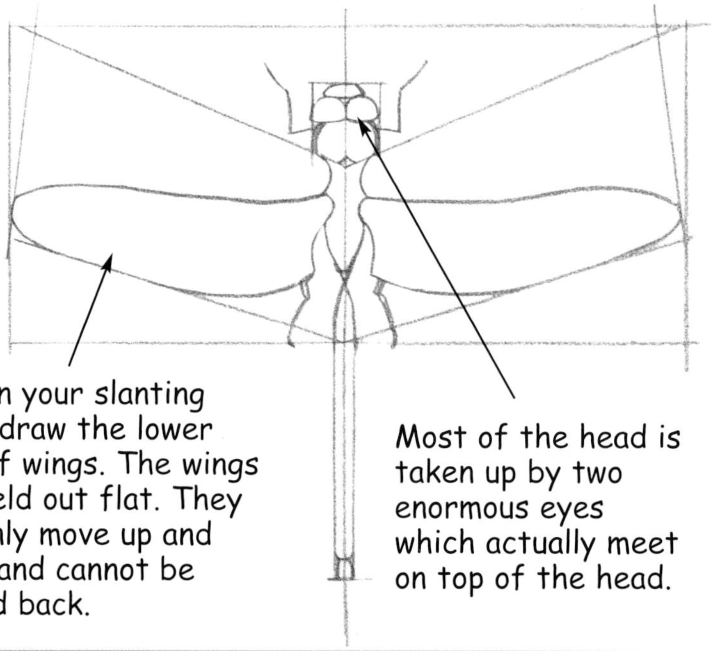

Within your slanting lines, draw the lower pair of wings. The wings are held out flat. They can only move up and down and cannot be folded back.

Most of the head is taken up by two enormous eyes which actually meet on top of the head.

Add the second pair of wings. In flight, both pairs of wings beat at the same time. When the dragonfly makes a sharp turn you can actually hear the rattling sound as the front and back wings hit each other.

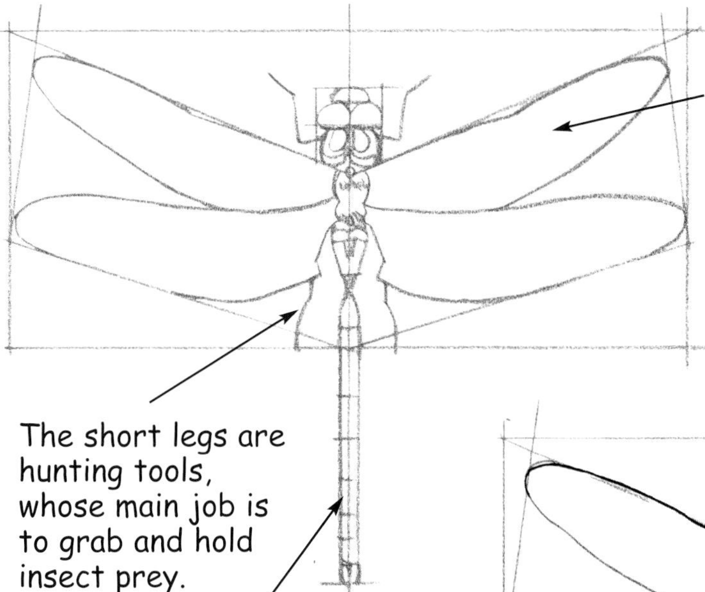

The short legs are hunting tools, whose main job is to grab and hold insect prey.

The body is patterned in bands. Dragonflies come in a wide range of colours, often with a metallic glint.

Finish off the head with a pair of short feelers. The head has strong biting jaws.

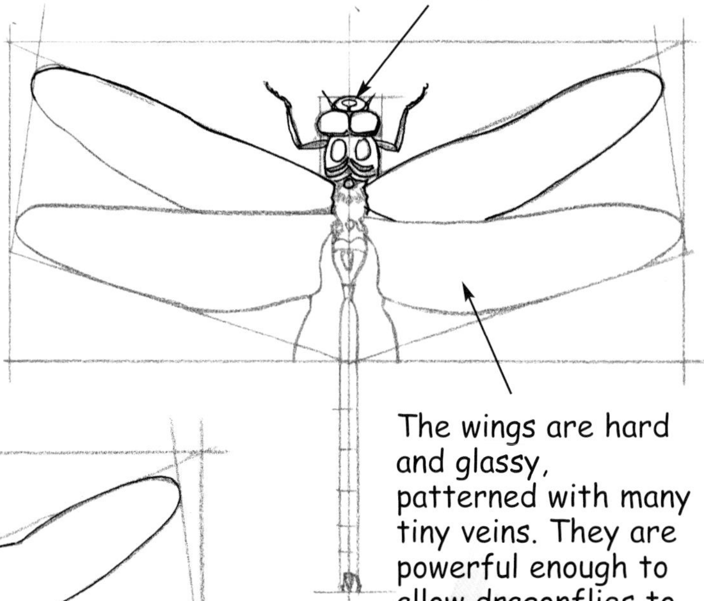

The wings are hard and glassy, patterned with many tiny veins. They are powerful enough to allow dragonflies to reach speeds of up to 30km/h.

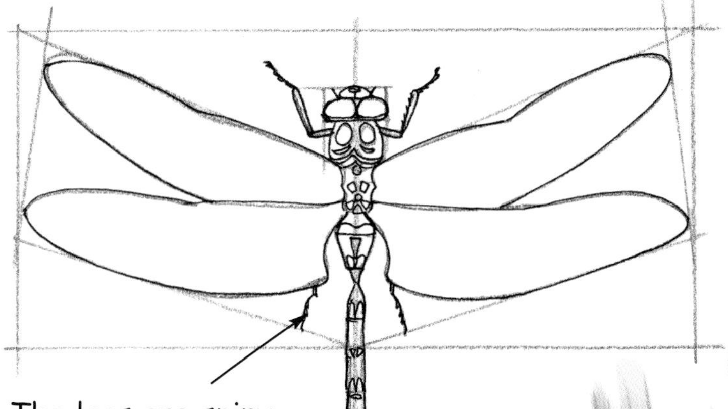

The legs are spiny, not smooth, to give a good grip on insect prey. When you ink in the legs, a few short strokes of your pen will create the spiny effect.

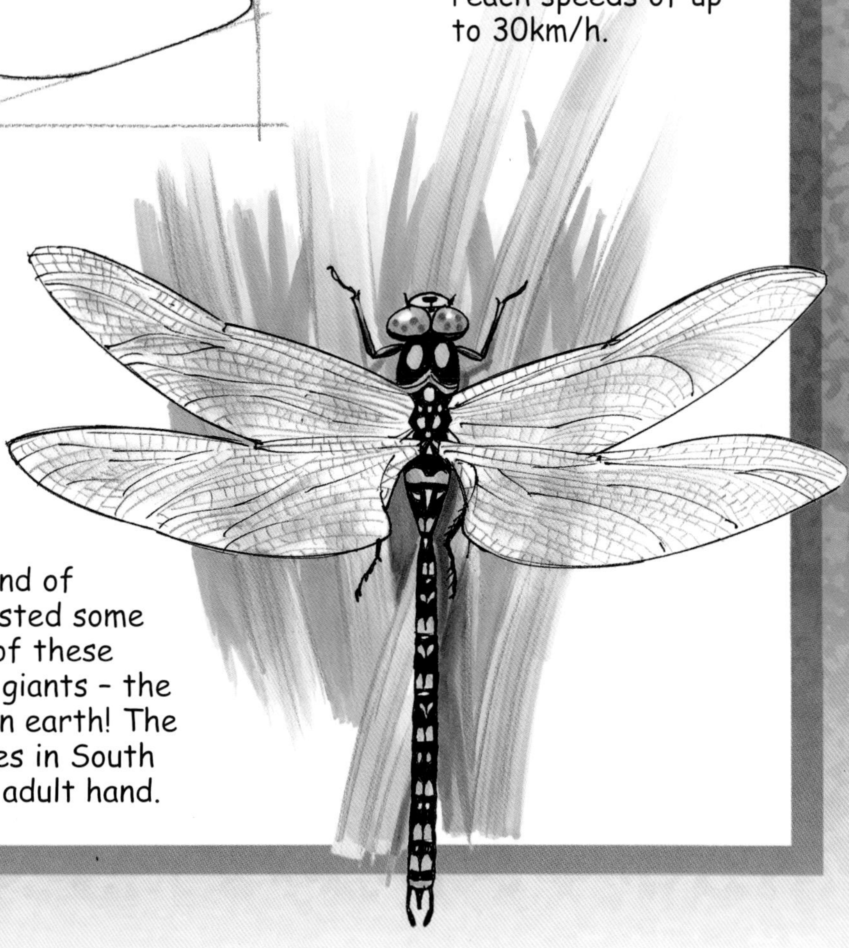

Dragonflies are the oldest kind of insect known today. They existed some 300 million years ago. Some of these prehistoric dragonflies were giants – the biggest insects ever to live on earth! The biggest modern dragonfly lives in South America. It is the size of an adult hand.

Bush Cricket

Crickets are famous for their loud chirruping 'song'. This is made by scraping the hard edges of the front wings against each other – rather like drawing a bow across violin strings. Bush Crickets are sometimes called Long-horned Grasshoppers, from their remarkably long feelers.

Start with this boat shape, and mark off a line at the front for the head.

Slanting lines create the huge back legs, which stick up above the insect's back.

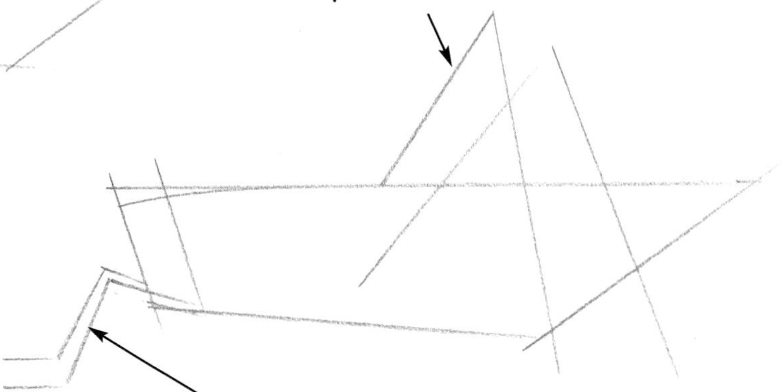

Draw in the front legs as simple lines. These legs are not just used for walking – they also contain the cricket's ears!

A slanting line across the centre of the body forms the base of the wing, which is held flat across the body.

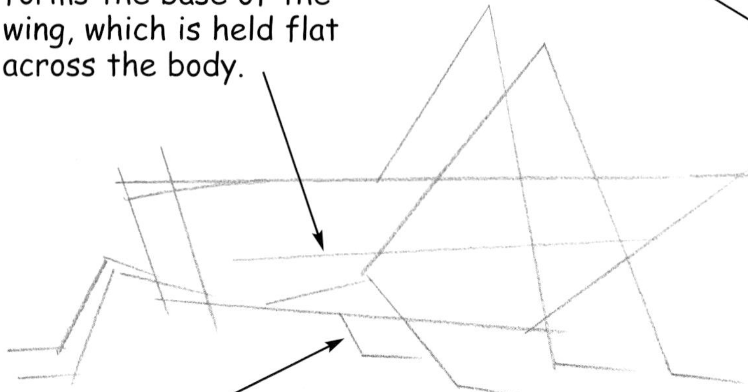

The second pair of legs points backwards.

Add two long, curving lines for the feelers. These are used to taste and to smell things.

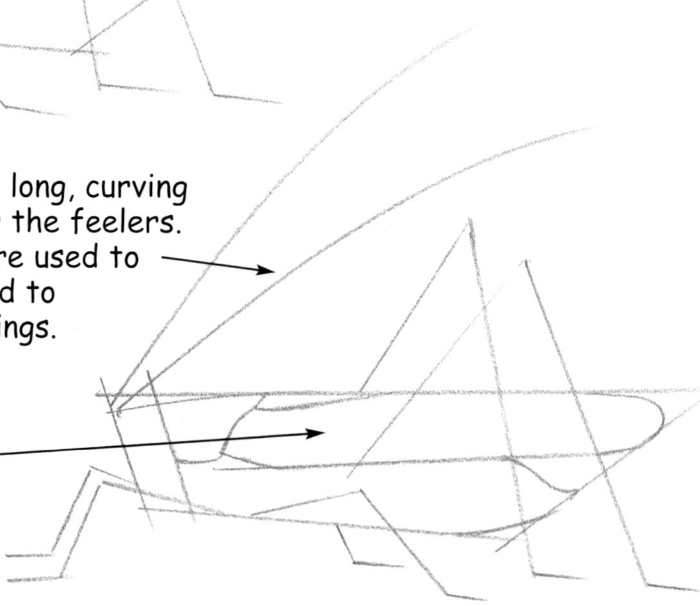

Now you can draw in the wings, rounding off the ends. Note that the wings stick out well beyond the end of the body.

Finish drawing the hind legs. These are long and strong, with big muscular thighs to power the cricket's mighty leaps.

These curving lines mark sections of the body.

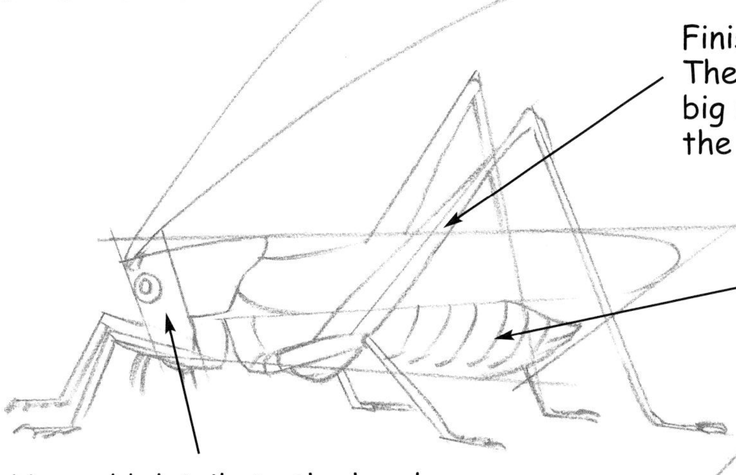

Now add details to the head. The eyes are large, and so are the jaws, which are designed for chewing plant food. The mouth-parts are partly hidden by the front legs.

A protective 'shield' lies behind the head, just in front of the wings.

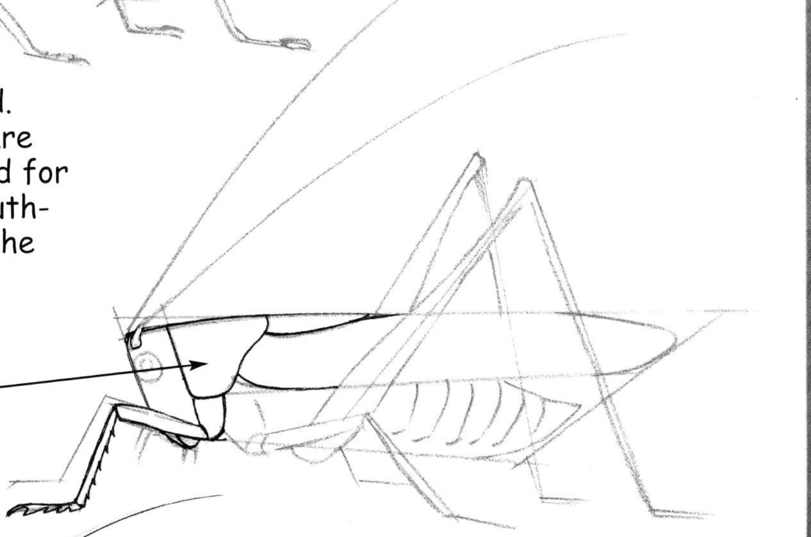

Wings and legs work together. The hindlegs provide power for the take-off, so the cricket is airborne before its wings have to start working.

As you ink in the long thin legs, mark in short stiff hairs on the edges of the lower sections.

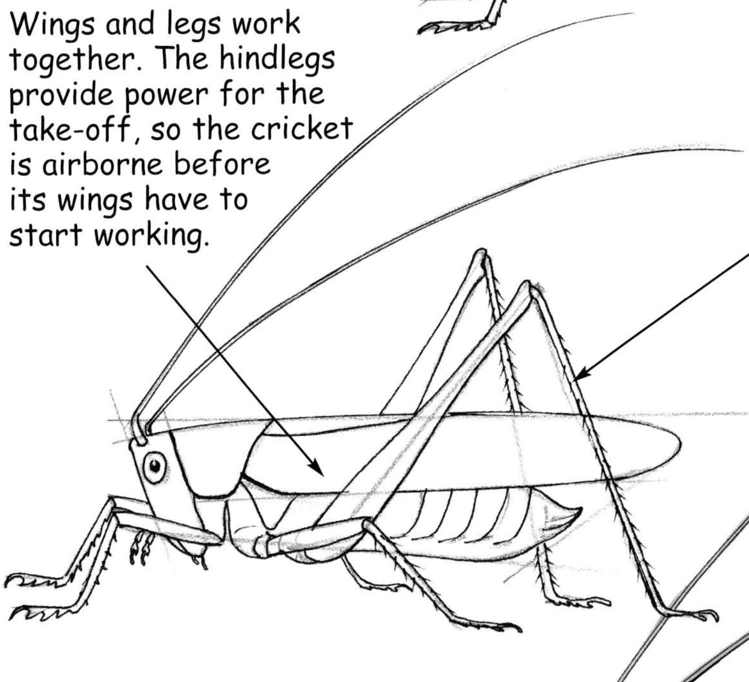

You can tell the cricket family from the grasshopper family by the length of their feelers – true grasshoppers have short feelers. Bush Crickets form a large family. There are 16,000 different kinds, some small, some as big as a hamster.

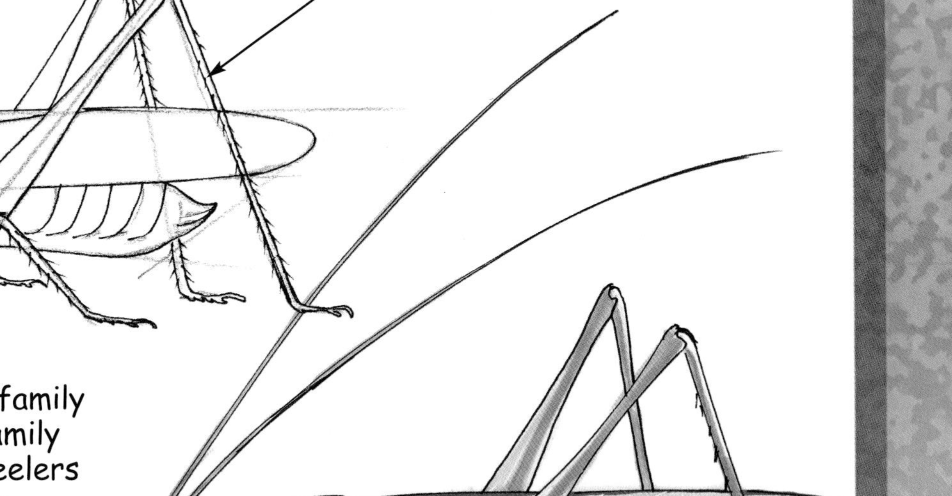

Centipede

The name 'centipede' means 'a hundred legs', but that isn't quite right. Different kinds of centipedes may have as many as 170 pairs of legs, or as few as 15 pairs. This tells us at once that the centipede is not a member of the insect family, for all insects have six legs.

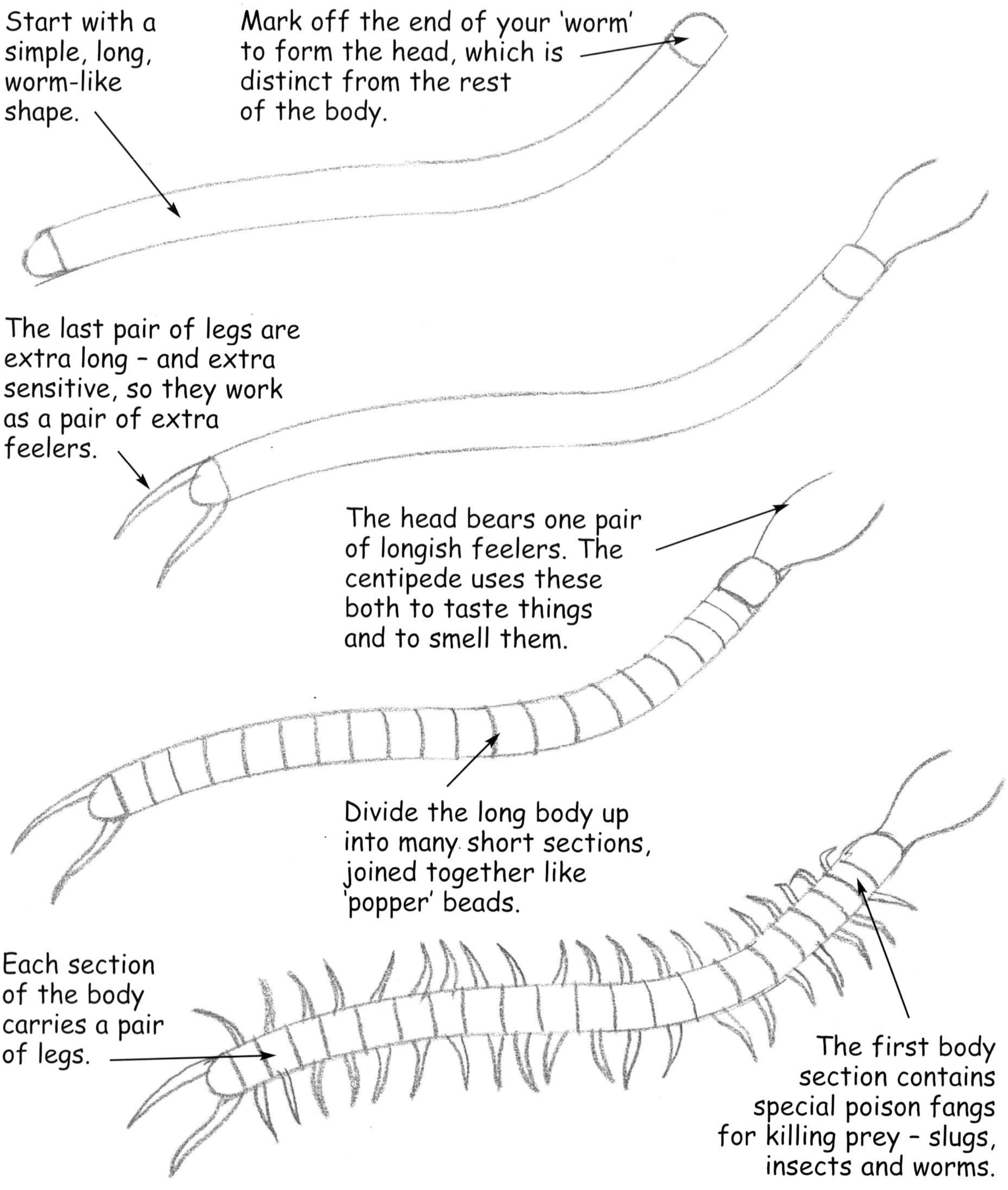

Start with a simple, long, worm-like shape.
Mark off the end of your 'worm' to form the head, which is distinct from the rest of the body.
The last pair of legs are extra long – and extra sensitive, so they work as a pair of extra feelers.
The head bears one pair of longish feelers. The centipede uses these both to taste things and to smell them.
Divide the long body up into many short sections, joined together like 'popper' beads.
Each section of the body carries a pair of legs.
The first body section contains special poison fangs for killing prey – slugs, insects and worms.

Each body section is covered in a hard 'armour' of horny skin. As the centipede grows, this armour gets too tight and has to be shed.

You can't see them from this angle, but the head bears three pairs of jaws.

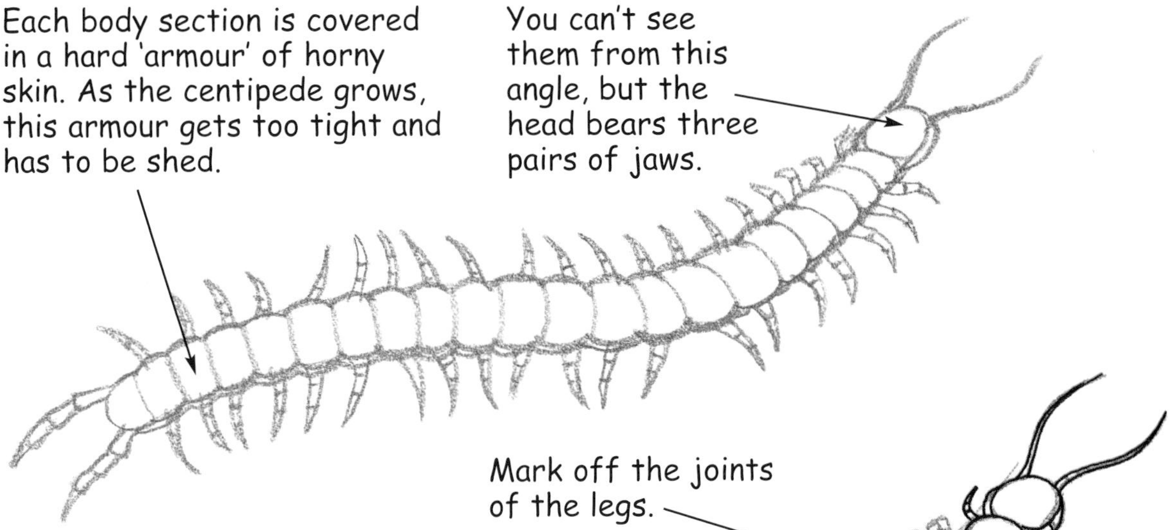

Mark off the joints of the legs.

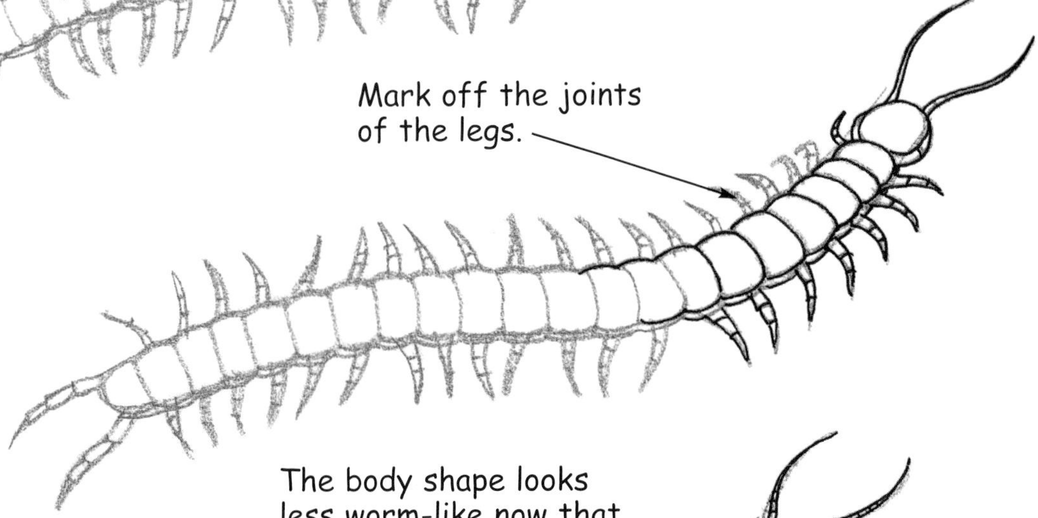

The body shape looks less worm-like now that it is broken up into its rounded sections.

Ink in the outlines of each joint separately to show how they fit together.

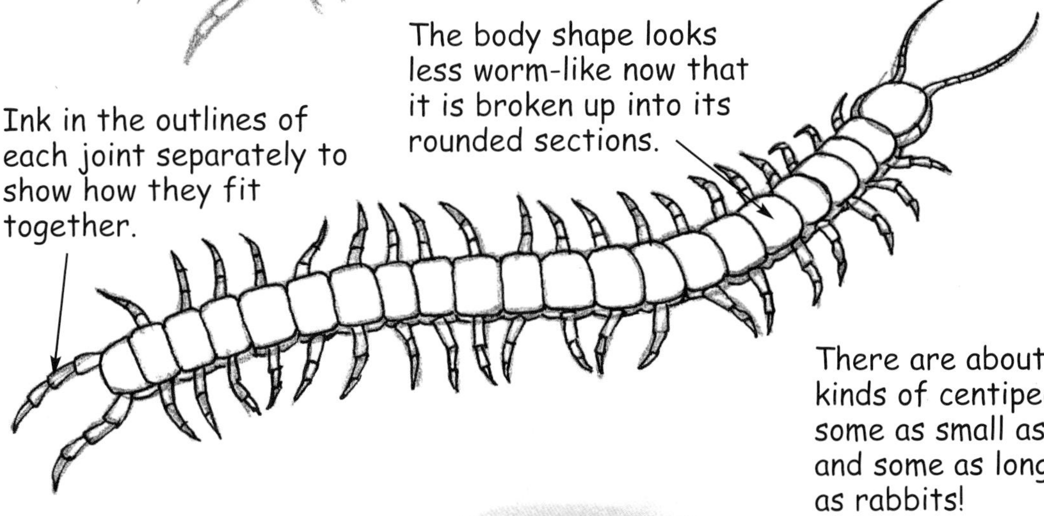

There are about 3,000 kinds of centipede, some as small as ants – and some as long as rabbits!

Centipedes and millipedes are often confused, but they are not very closely related. You can tell them apart by the legs: millipedes have two pairs on each body section, centipedes only one pair.

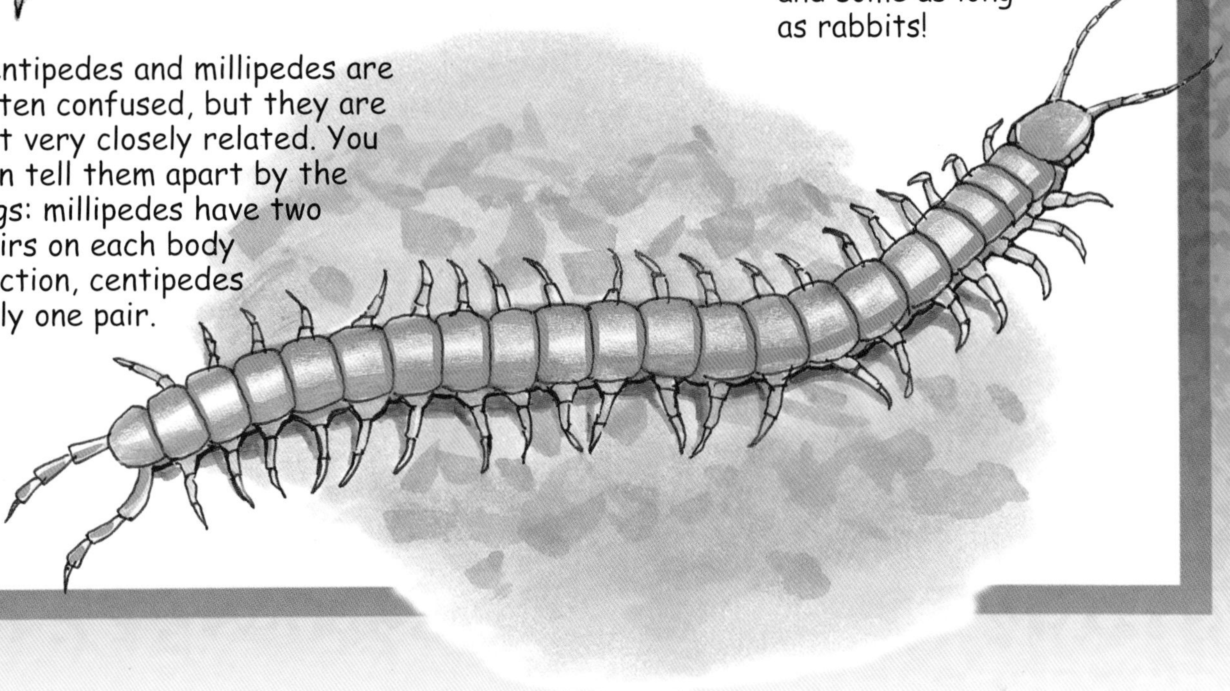

Stag Beetle

Beetles come in more different kinds than any other living creature. The Stag Beetle is one of the most handsome. It is a big, unusually powerful insect, about the size of a mouse (minus the tail!). It gets its name from the male's enormous jaws which look a bit like a stag's antlers.

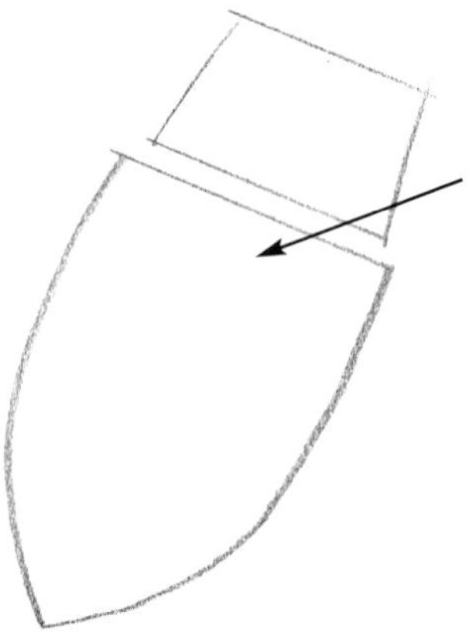

Like all insects, beetles are made up of three sections: the head, and two body parts. Start with these two shapes for the body.

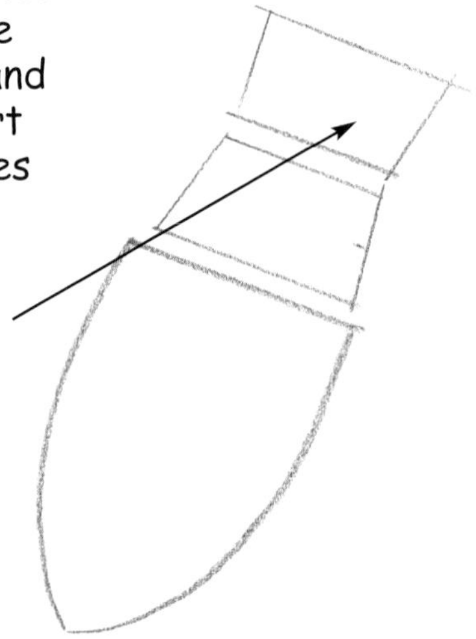

Add this shape for the head, and most of the beetle is completed.

Now draw the enormous jaws that give this beetle its name.

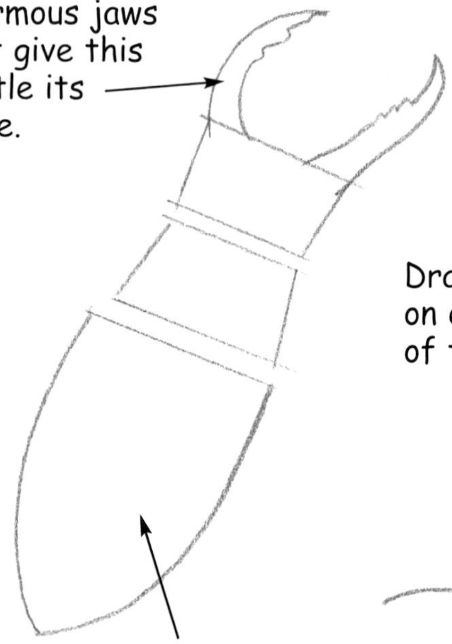

The wings lie over this part of the body – but you can't see them. The front wings are not used for flight, but form a protective cover for the rear, flying wings.

These tough-looking jaws are actually too weak to bite with, and not even useful for eating. Their jaws are only used for wrestling with other males at mating time.

Draw a feeler on either side of the head.

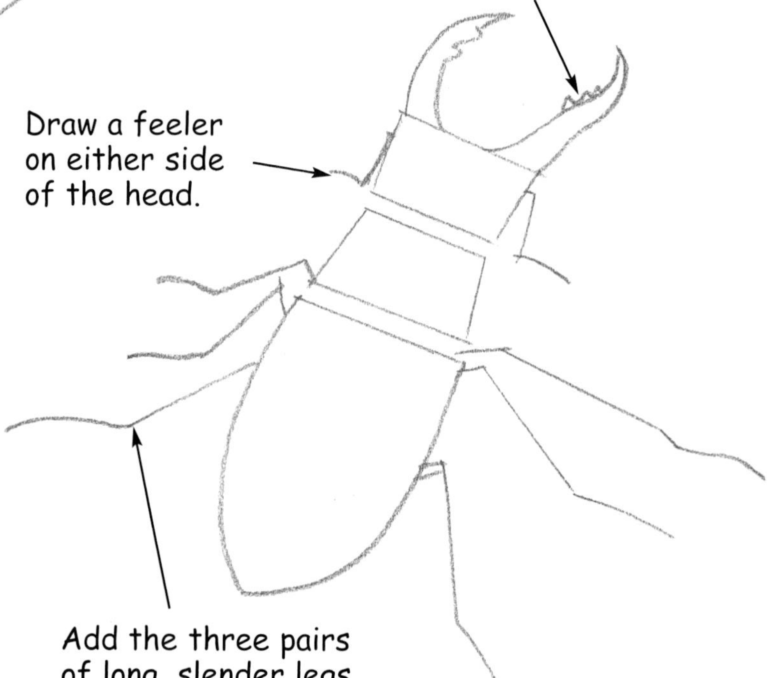

Add the three pairs of long, slender legs.

All three pairs of legs are attached to the front part of the body.

Add short, feathery hairs to the ends of the feelers.

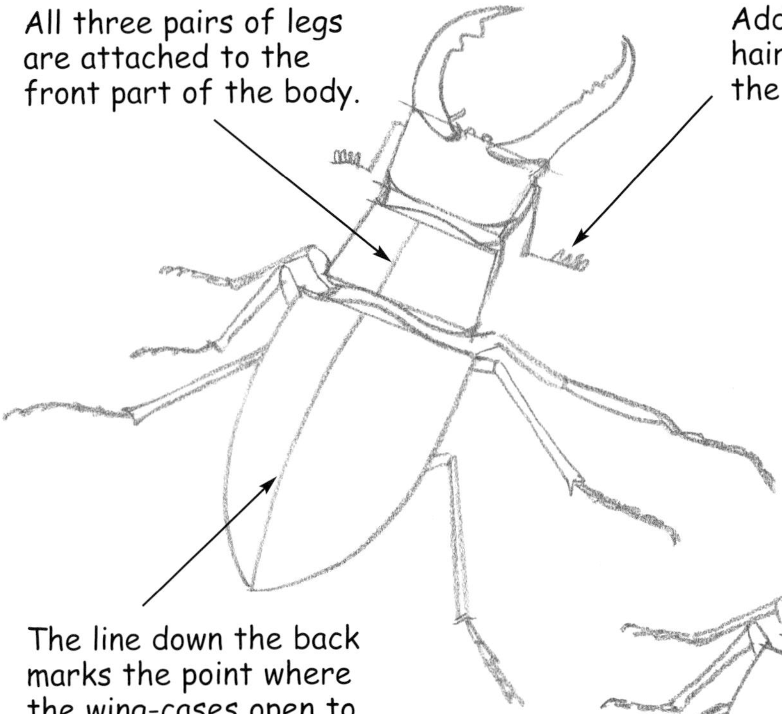

The line down the back marks the point where the wing-cases open to release the wings for flight.

Now shape the head. Notice how it narrows where it joins the body.

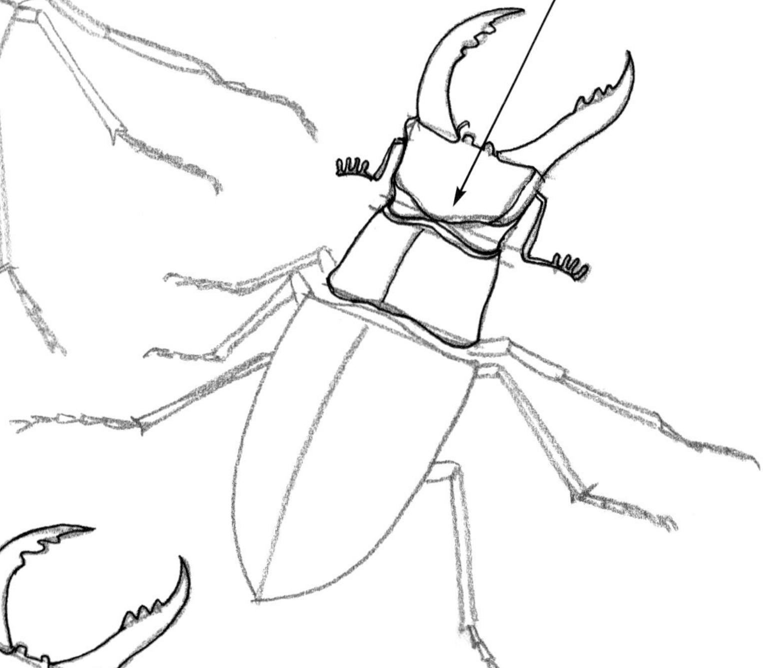

As with all insects, the legs end in two tiny claws.

Unlike ours, these jaws move sideways, instead of up and down.

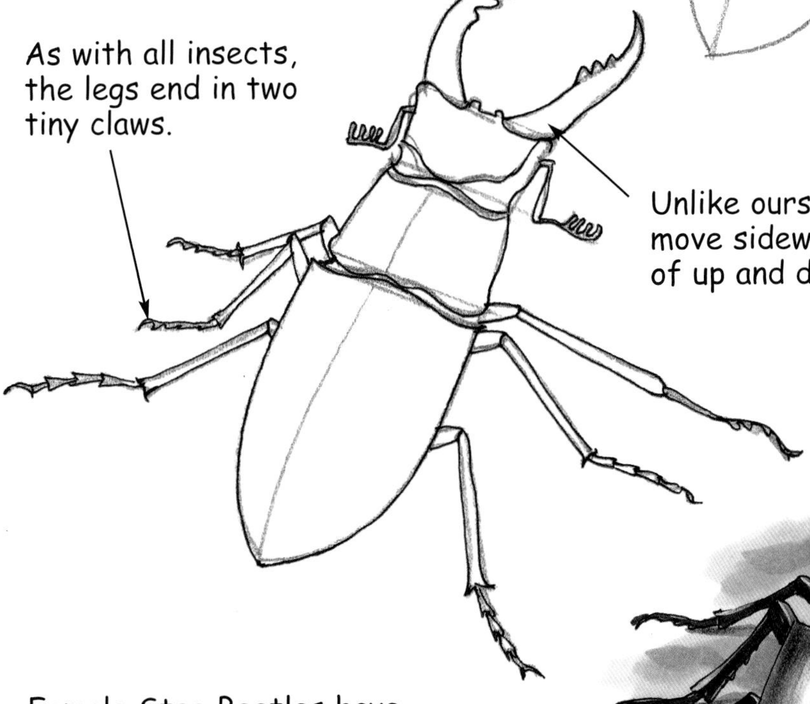

Female Stag Beetles have normal jaws without the impressive 'antlers' of the male. Surprisingly, this allows them to give you a nastier nip than the males!

Pond Skater

Pond skaters are common in pools and streams, where they hunt for small insect prey. They 'skate' over the surface of the water, without sinking or even getting wet. Only their feet touch the water, and these are too light to break through the surface.

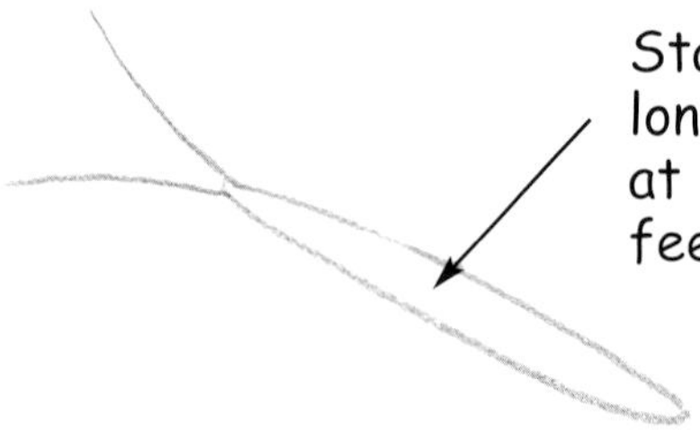

Start your drawing with the long, thin body, which tapers at each end. Add two long feelers at the front.

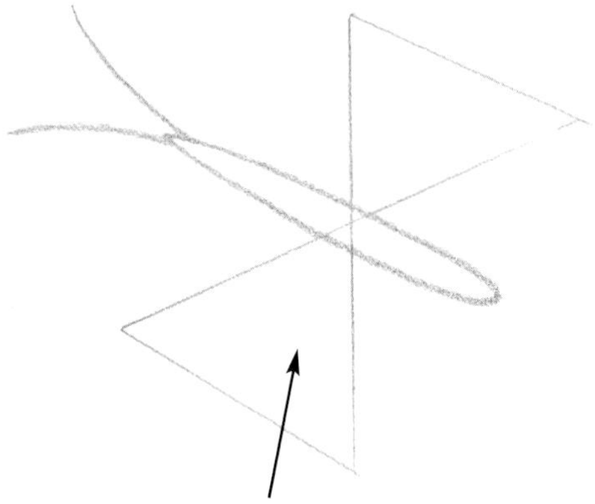

These two triangles are guidelines to show you where to position the middle and back pairs of legs.

The front legs are much shorter than the back ones.

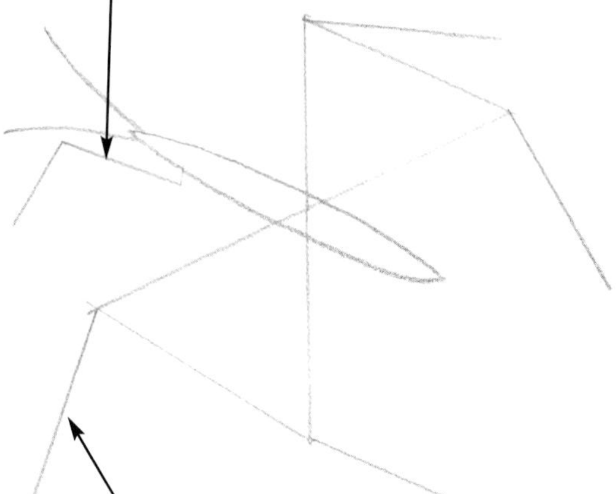

Now take a line beyond your triangles to add the next part of the long, slender legs.

The head is very small, so the large eyes bulge out on either side. Good eyesight is important to pond skaters, to help them spot their prey.

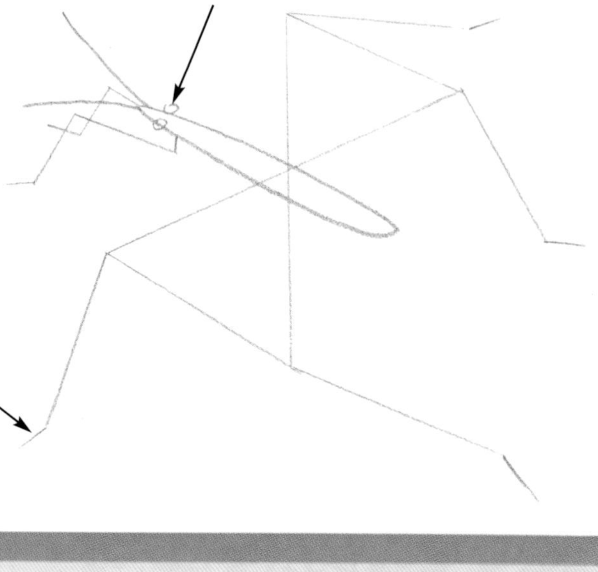

Add the last, short section to the legs. These are the only parts of the insect that touch the water.

If you watch a pond skater, you will see the tiny dents in the water where the claws touch it without ever breaking the surface. Draw small ovals under the feet to mark these dents.

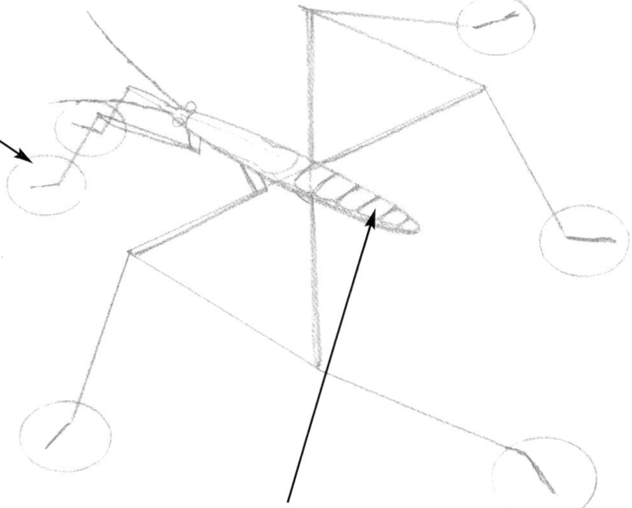

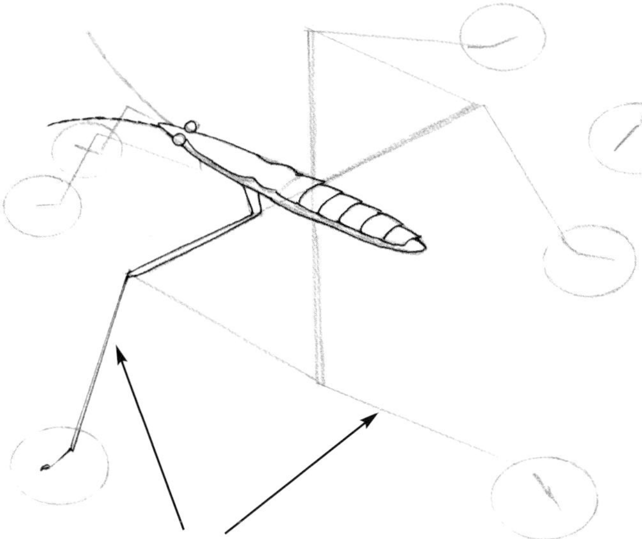

Draw bands across the back part of the body, to show how it is made up of several sections.

The two longer pairs of legs move the pond skater along. The middle pair work like oars, rowing the body forward, while the back pair are used for steering.

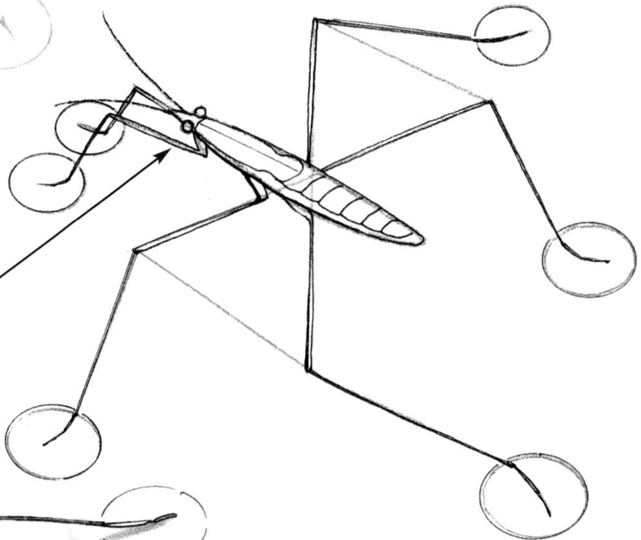

The shorter, front pair of legs are hunting weapons. They are used to grab and hold on to prey.

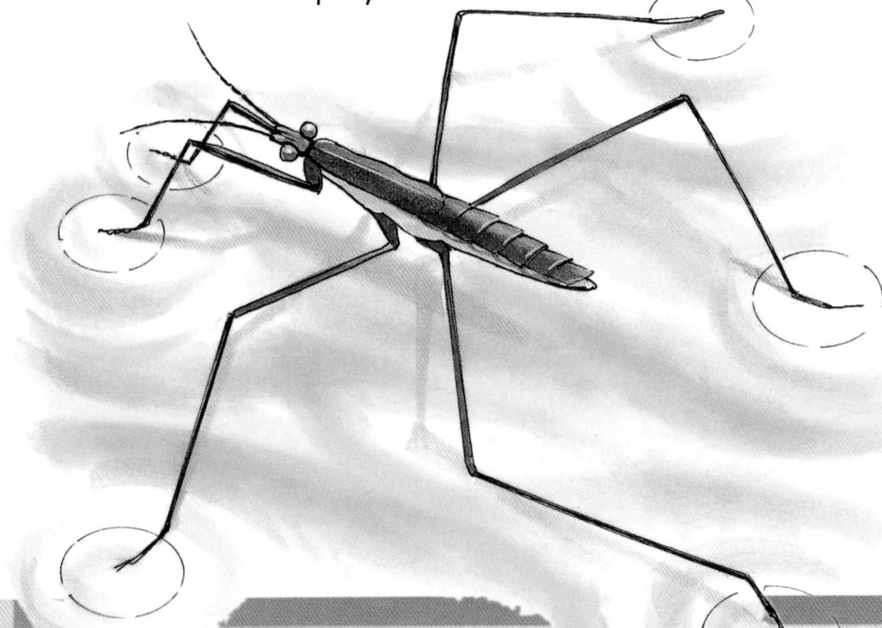

Pond skaters stay dry even if they dive under the water. Their bodies are covered with very fine, downy fur. This forms a waterproof suit, for it traps a thin layer of air which the water cannot pass through.

Spider

There are some 40,000 different kinds of spider, and they all spin silk. Most weave it into webs to catch insects. Webs range from the well-known round orb webs to simple tubes, complicated funnels, running trip-wires or even, in the case of the bolas spider, a 'lasso' to rope its prey.

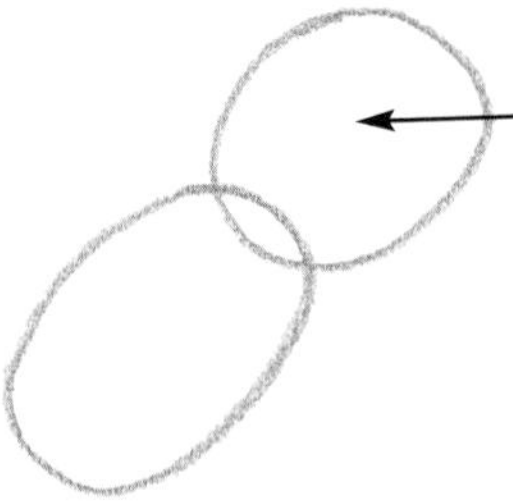

These two shapes form the body. Like insects, a spider's body is in two parts. But, unlike insects, it has no separate head.

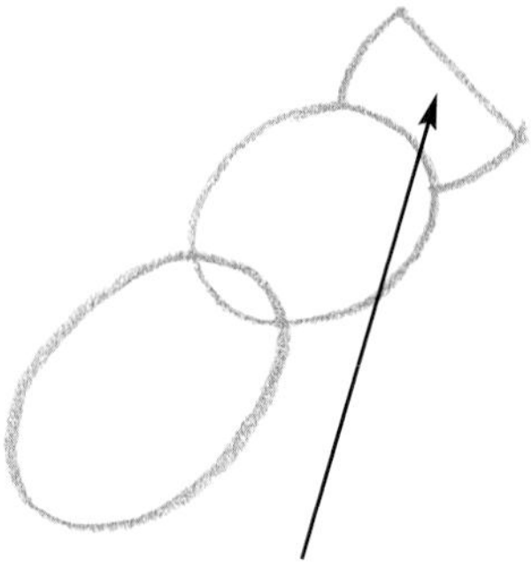

Add this half-moon shape to mark where the eyes and jaws fit on the front of the body.

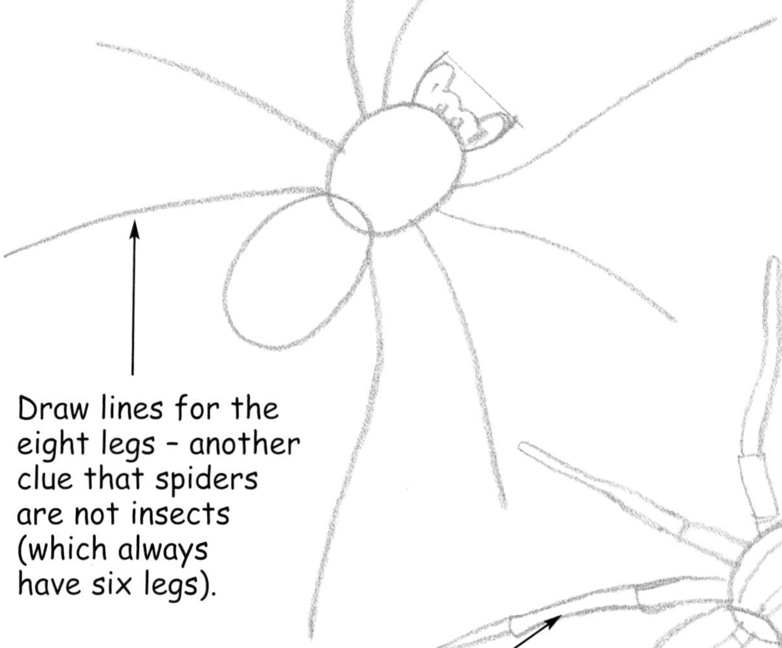

Draw lines for the eight legs – another clue that spiders are not insects (which always have six legs).

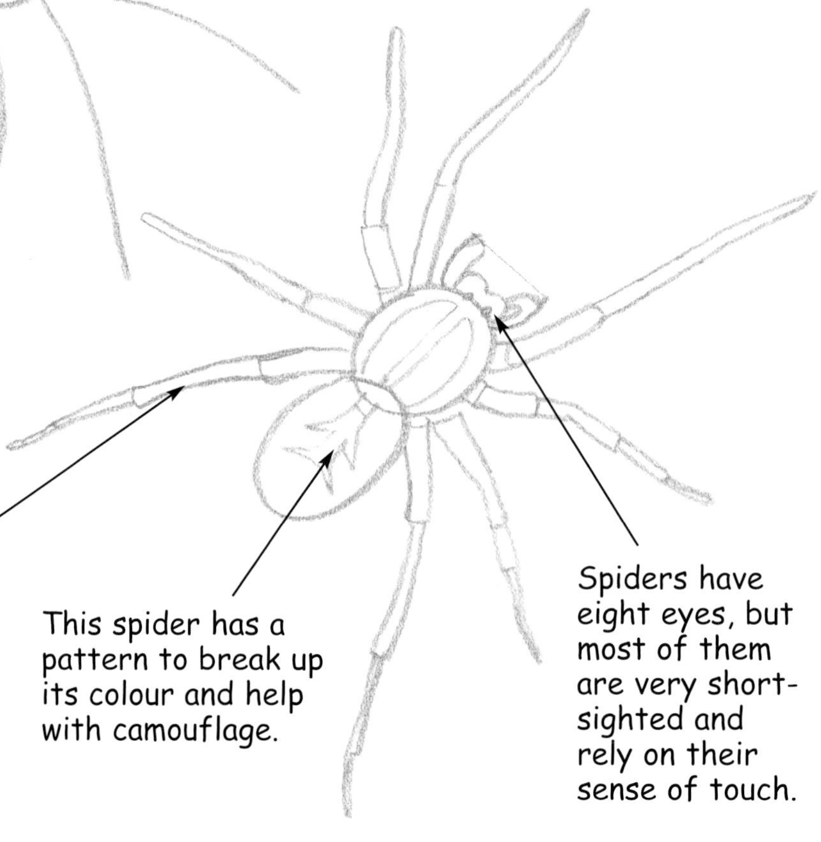

Build up your lines into legs, marking out the joints. Just like our legs, the top sections are thickest, the lower ones more slender.

This spider has a pattern to break up its colour and help with camouflage.

Spiders have eight eyes, but most of them are very short-sighted and rely on their sense of touch.

Each leg is made up of several tiny sections (you don't need to show all of them!) and ends in tiny claws.

Unlike insects, spiders have no feelers. These two short leg-like parts at the front of the body are palps, special sensitive mouth-parts which act rather like feelers.

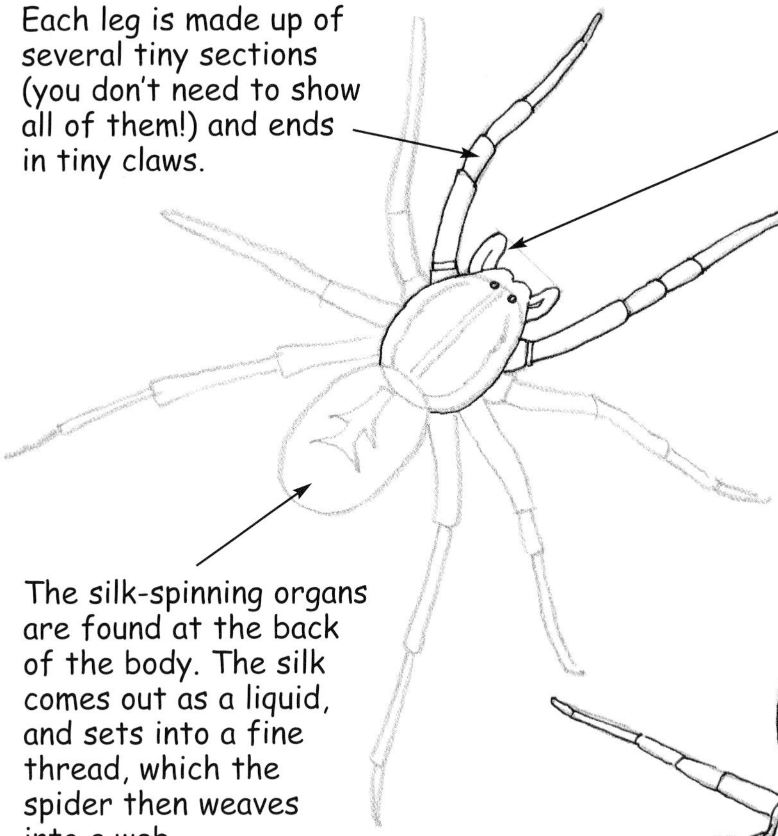

The silk-spinning organs are found at the back of the body. The silk comes out as a liquid, and sets into a fine thread, which the spider then weaves into a web.

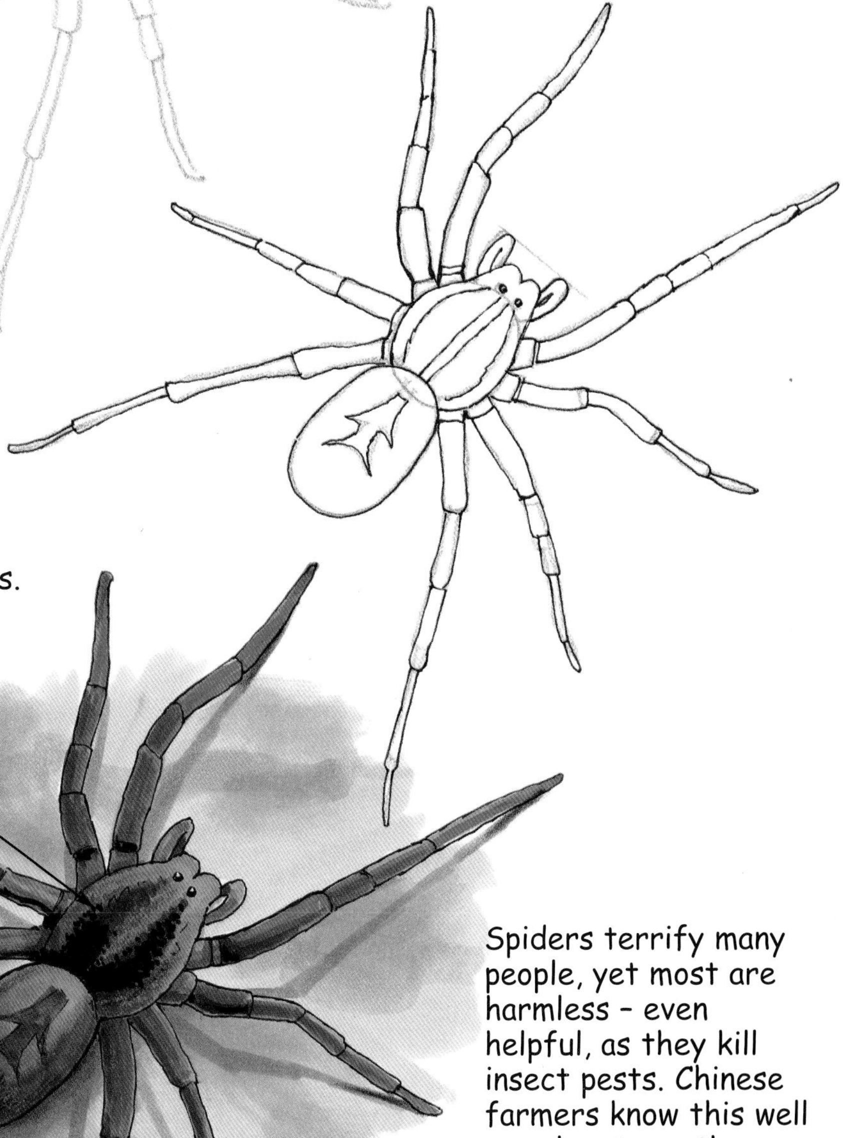

Most spiders are a dark, dull colour to help them hide away in unlit corners. Some poisonous spiders are brightly coloured, as a warning signal to predators.

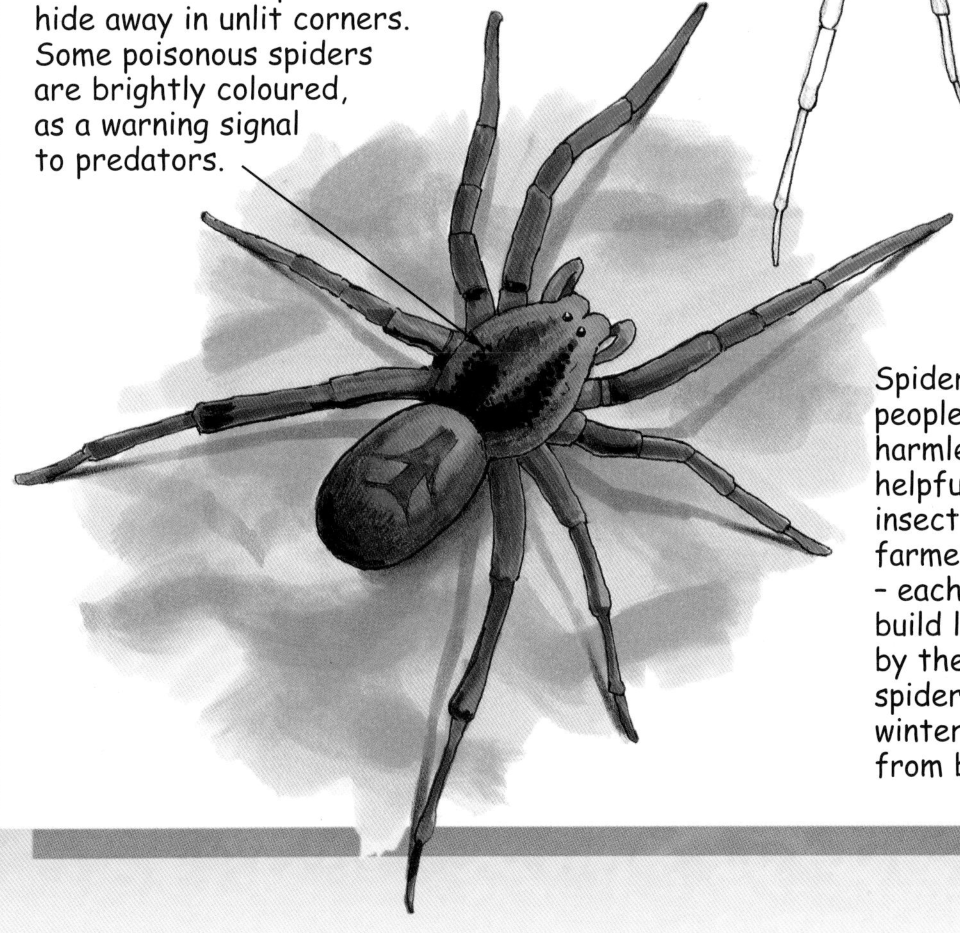

Spiders terrify many people, yet most are harmless – even helpful, as they kill insect pests. Chinese farmers know this well – each autumn they build little spider-huts by their fields, helping spiders survive the winter to guard crops from bugs next spring.

Devil's Coach Horse

When this beetle faces a threat, it threatens back! It snaps its jaws (it can give quite a nasty nip), curves the end of its body upwards – and then fires a 'stink bomb' from its rear end. The way its body rises up reminded people of a rearing horse – which explains the name.

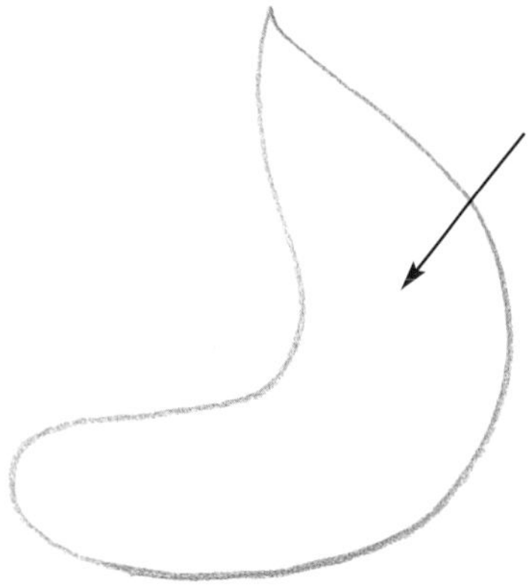

This shape forms the long, narrow body, with the back end raised ready for self-defence. This position also makes the beetle look bigger, helping to frighten off enemies.

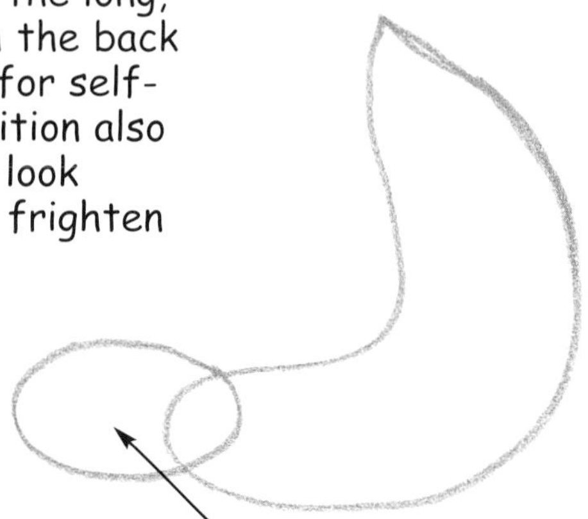

Add an oval for the smaller front section of the body.

Another oval forms the head. Now you have the three basic parts that make up all insects.

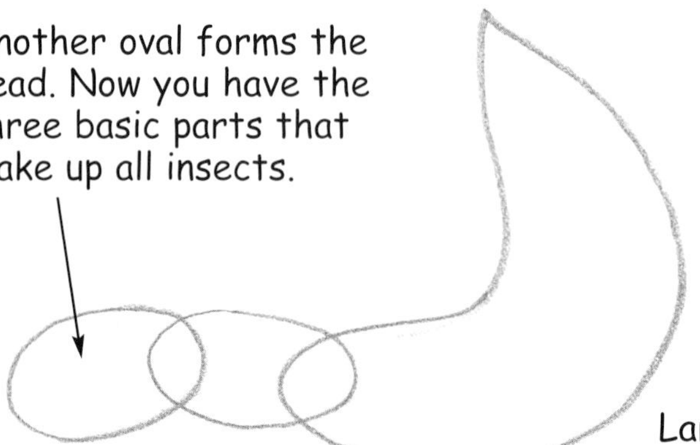

Large eyes mean good eyesight and help this hunting beetle to find its prey.

The large jaws are shaped (and used) like a pair of pincers. When the beetle is alarmed, it opens its jaws wide and snaps at anything that approaches.

Like all insects, this beetle has six jointed legs – though you can't see all of them from this angle.

Use a feathery line to draw the feelers, to show that they are made up of many little sections.

Unlike many beetles, this one has very short wing-cases, which cover less than half the body. They are squared off at the ends.

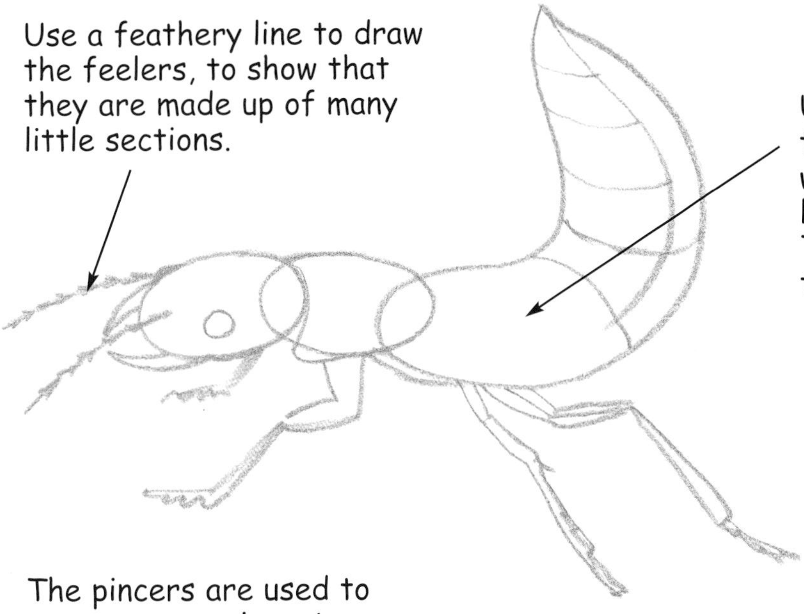

The pincers are used to tear up prey – insects, spiders and other small creepy crawlies. The beetle usually drags its dinner under cover before pulling it apart and eating it.

This tough, shield-shaped shell protects the front part of the body.

Note that the end of the body is made up of different segments.

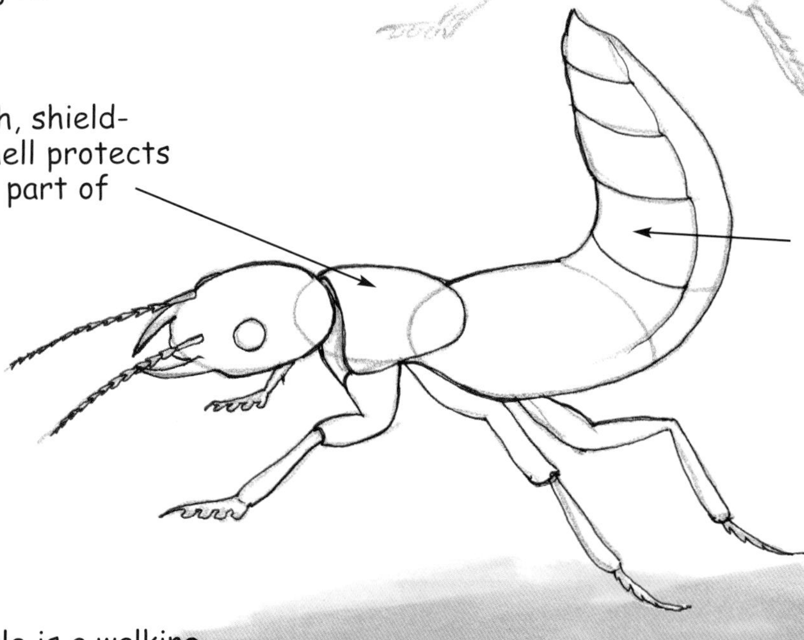

This beetle is a walking chemical factory, with a choice of stink bombs for defence. It can spray a foul gas from its rear end, or squirt a nasty liquid from both ends at once.

Wasp

Everybody knows wasps, but not many people like them. They sting, and they get into the jam on picnics. But they do have their good points. They kill insect pests, such as flies, and they act as refuse collectors, eating up rubbish like rotten fruit and decaying flesh.

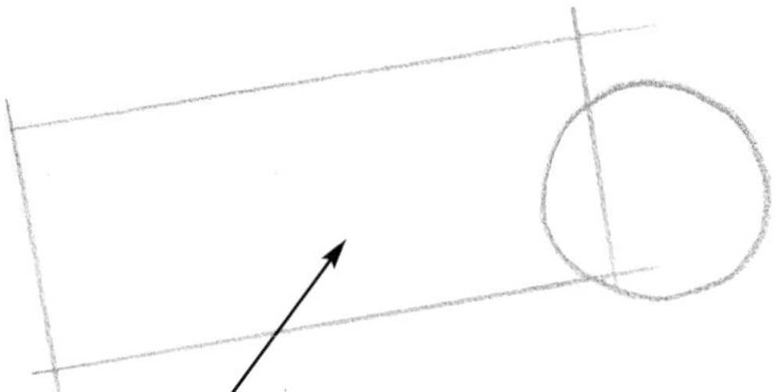

These two simple shapes form the two sections of the body.

A big triangle forms guidelines for the upper wing.

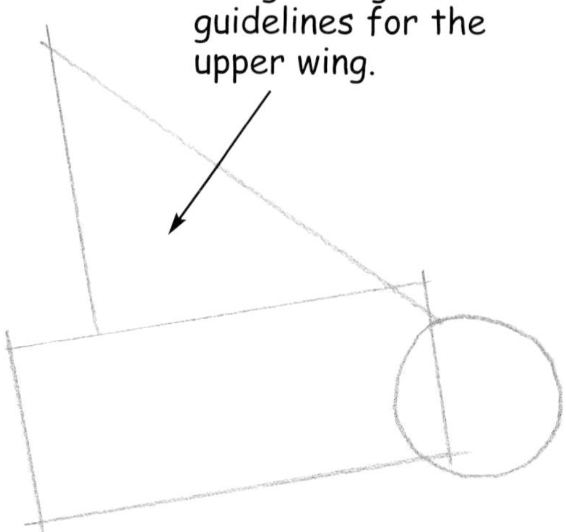

Add guidelines for the legs, and make a line where the upper wing will end.

The head is fairly large, long and can turn freely around.

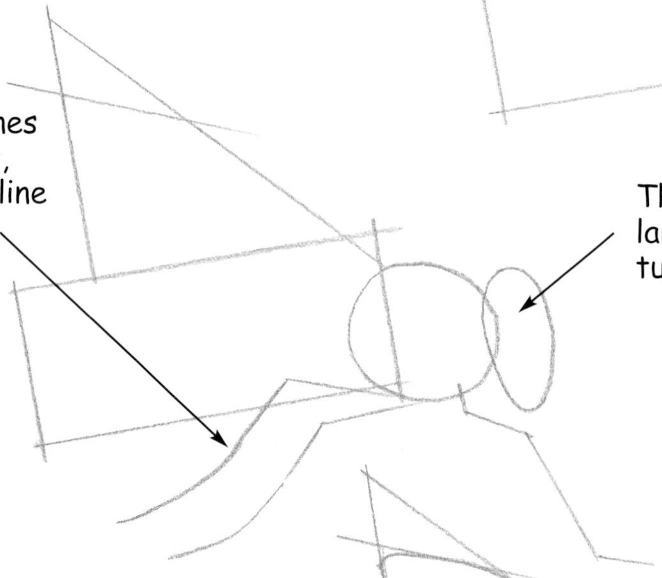

Add two downward-pointing feelers. These are very sensitive, and allow the wasp to smell food from a long way away.

Wasps have two pairs of wings. Draw in the pair on this side. The upper wing is bigger than the lower one, and provides most of the power for flight.

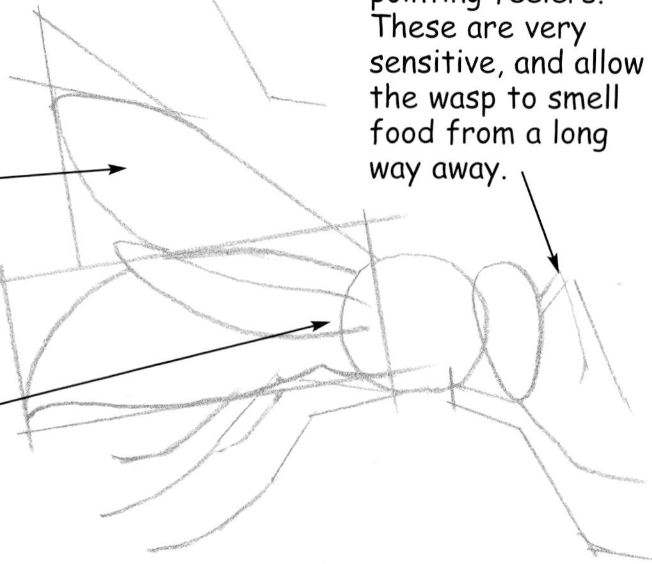

A wasp's body narrows at the point where the two parts join. This is typical of wasps – so we call people with very slender waists 'wasp-waisted'.

Draw the stripes on the second part of the body. Note that they are not straight bands, but long wavy patches.

Add the large eyes. Unlike our eyes, these are made up of many lenses, so that each eye sees many little views instead of just one.

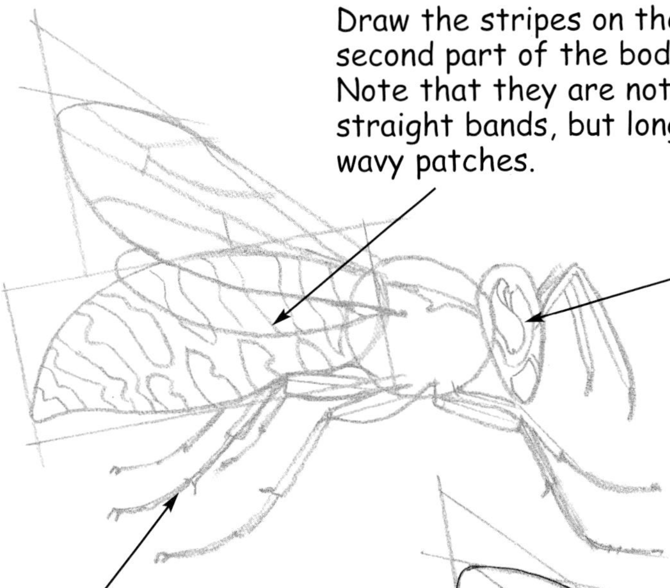

Using your guidelines, draw in the legs, taking care with the separate sections.

The wings are transparent, so you can see the veins inside. The edges of the upper and lower wings are 'zipped' together by tiny hooks so that they work together.

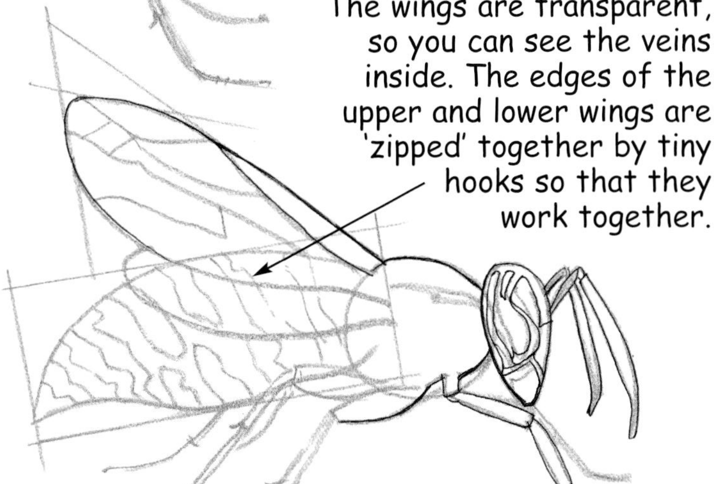

The head and front part of the body are covered with fine hairs. Use a very fine pen to sketch these in around the edges.

The sting is tucked away at the back of the body until needed.

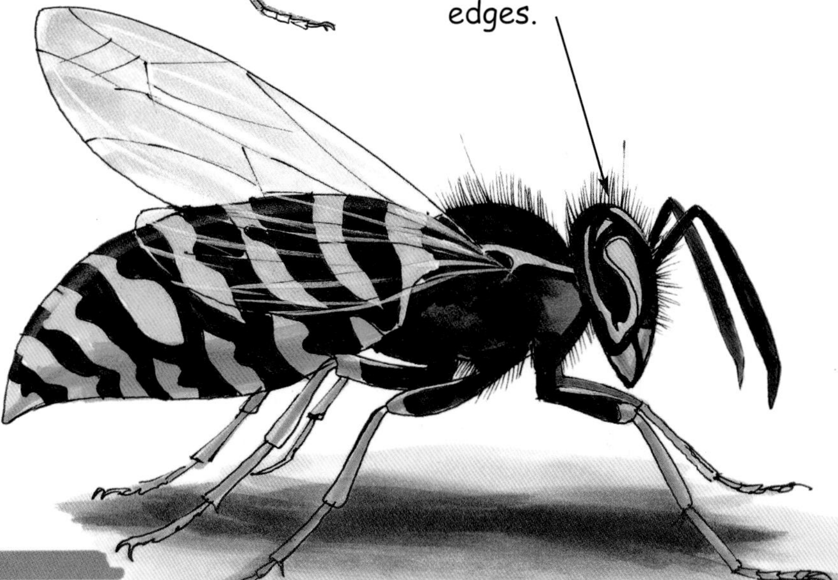

In nature, black and yellow are colours which often serve as a 'Keep Off' sign, warning that the owner carries poison fangs or a sting.

Longhorn Beetle

Longhorn beetles are vegetarians, eating flowers and leaves. Their larvae (caterpillars) eat wood. Though one larva doesn't eat much on its own, a crowd of them can damage a forest seriously – especially since they spend three or more years wood-chomping before they turn into adults.

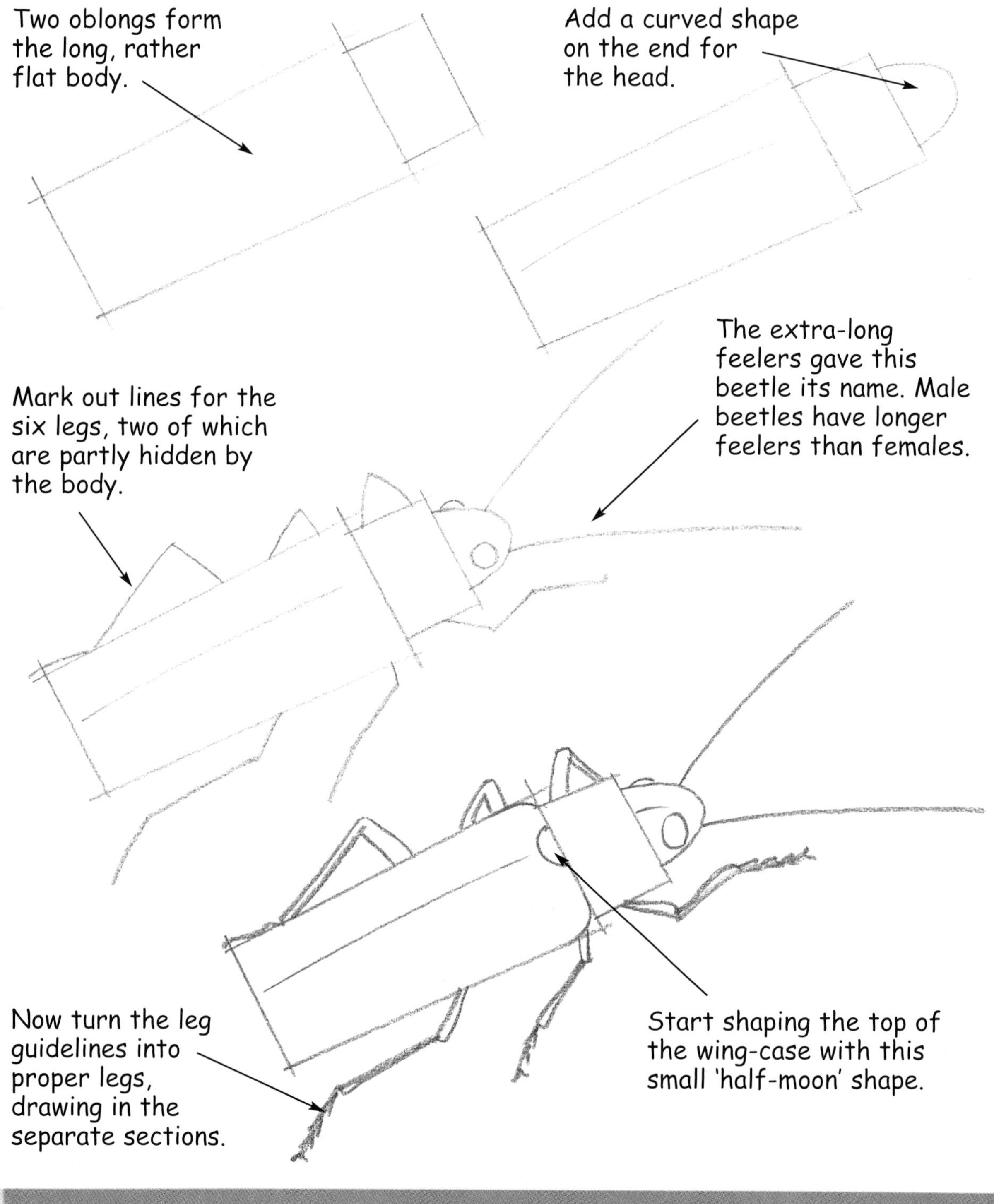
Two oblongs form the long, rather flat body.
Add a curved shape on the end for the head.
Mark out lines for the six legs, two of which are partly hidden by the body.
The extra-long feelers gave this beetle its name. Male beetles have longer feelers than females.
Now turn the leg guidelines into proper legs, drawing in the separate sections.
Start shaping the top of the wing-case with this small 'half-moon' shape.

The wing-cases cover the whole lower body. Most, but not all, Longhorns have a working pair of wings tucked underneath these, and can fly.

Some members of the Longhorn family have feelers which are much longer than their own bodies.

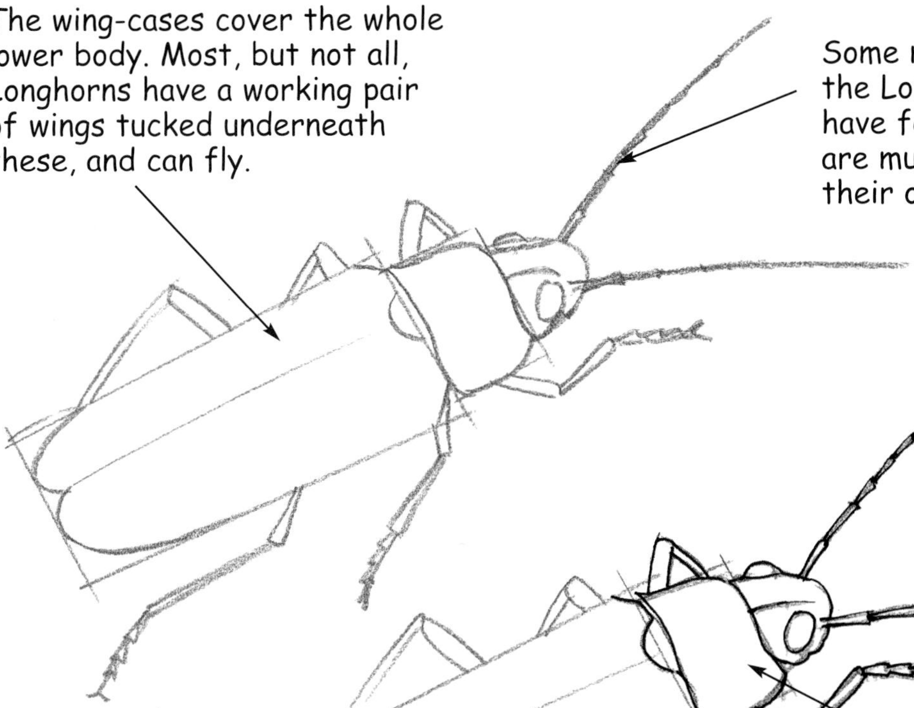

The front section of the body is protected by a hard shell.

Now finish off the wing-cases by rounding off their ends.

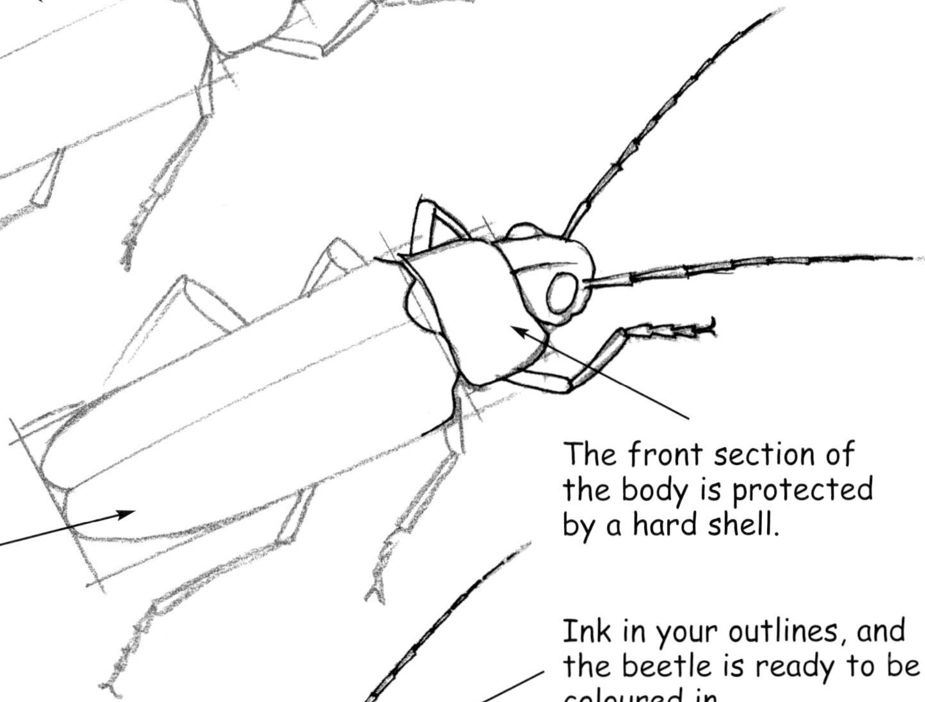

Ink in your outlines, and the beetle is ready to be coloured in.

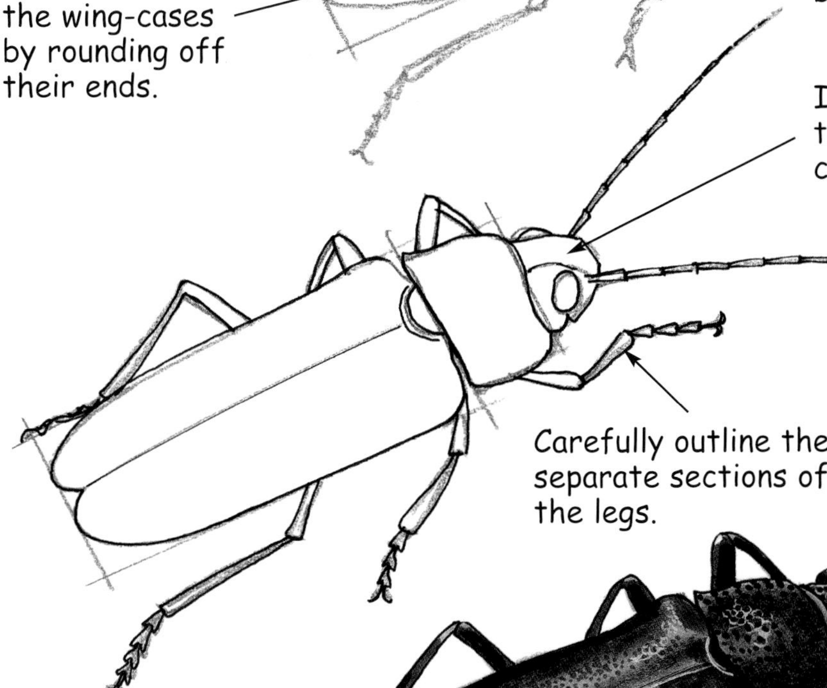

Carefully outline the separate sections of the legs.

There are many kinds of Longhorn Beetles. Some wear drab camouflage colours, but others are very colourful.

Scorpion

Scorpions are deadly hunters, with poisoned weapons. Their bodies end in a long 'tail' with a sting at the end. This is used to kill small prey, but it is also for self-defence, so people sometimes get stung. Scorpion stings are very painful, and a few are poisonous enough to kill humans.

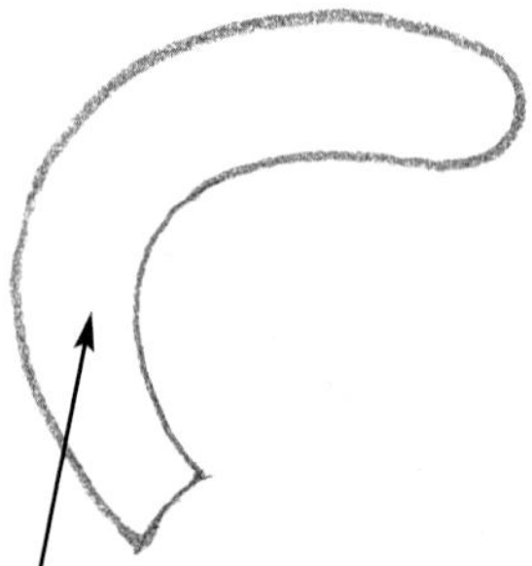

Start at the end, with the curved 'tail' – actually the end of the body.

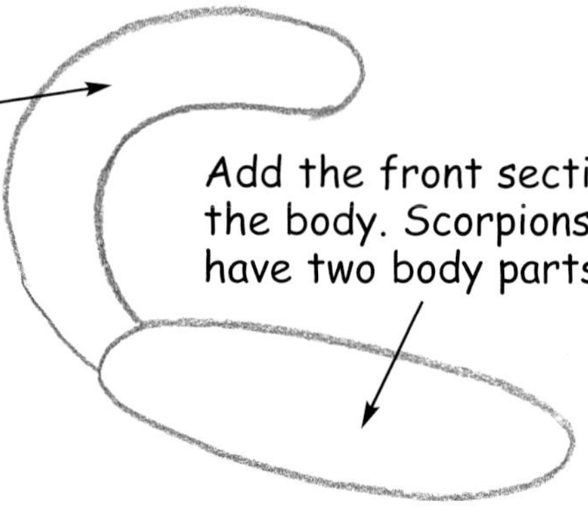

The 'tail' is held curved over the back, ready to bring its sting into action.

Add the front section of the body. Scorpions only have two body parts.

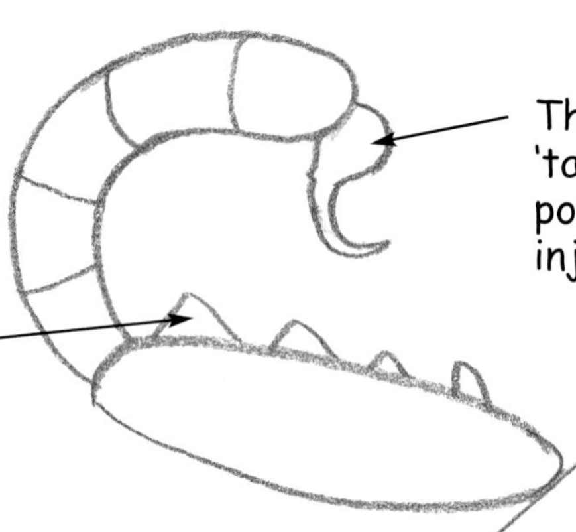

The sting at the end of the 'tail' ends in a fine curved point. It stabs a victim, then injects poison into the wound.

These are the tops of four legs, half-hidden by the body. Scorpions have eight legs, like spiders.

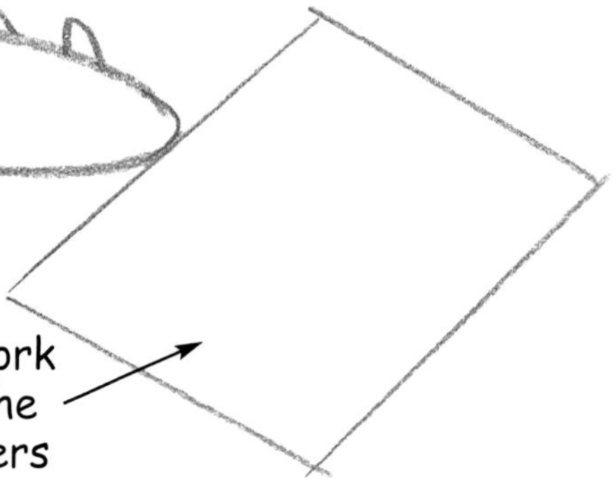

These four lines provide a framework for you to draw the large pair of pincers at the front.

The pincers look very much like a crab's claws. They are used to seize prey (insects and spiders). They also serve to cut up dinner afterwards.

The 'tail' (really the abdomen, or back part of the body) is made up of six rounded sections. The last one bears the sting.

Draw in the sections of the front part of the body. The front segment, which carries eyes and jaws, is the largest.

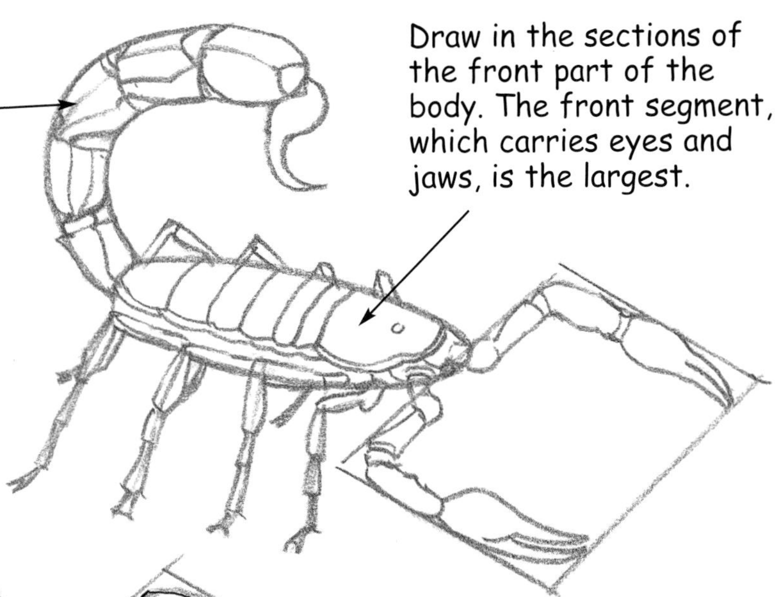

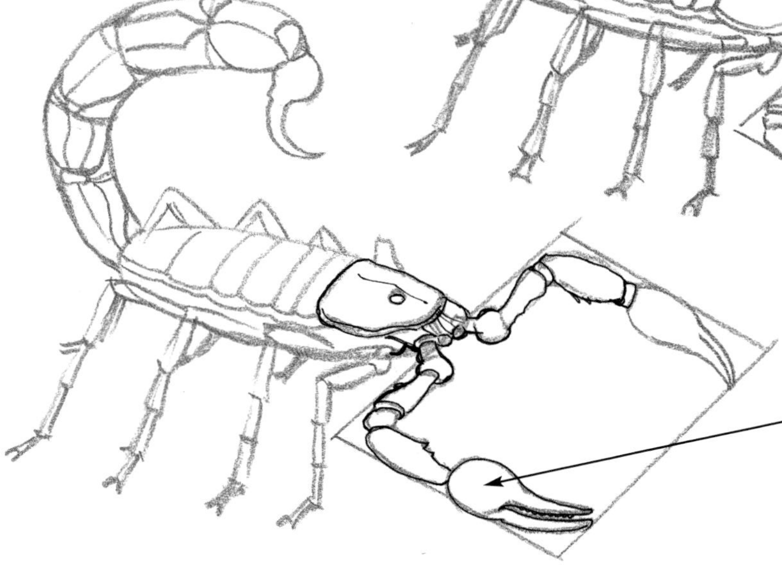

Once a victim is firmly gripped in these pincers, it has little chance of avoiding the sting. Death is quick, but dinner is leisurely. Scorpions are slow feeders, and may take more than an hour to eat a beetle.

The sting is usually carried 'at ease', point downwards. In attack or defence, the tail curves up to aim the sting at the victim.

Ink in your outlines, taking care to define the sections of the body.

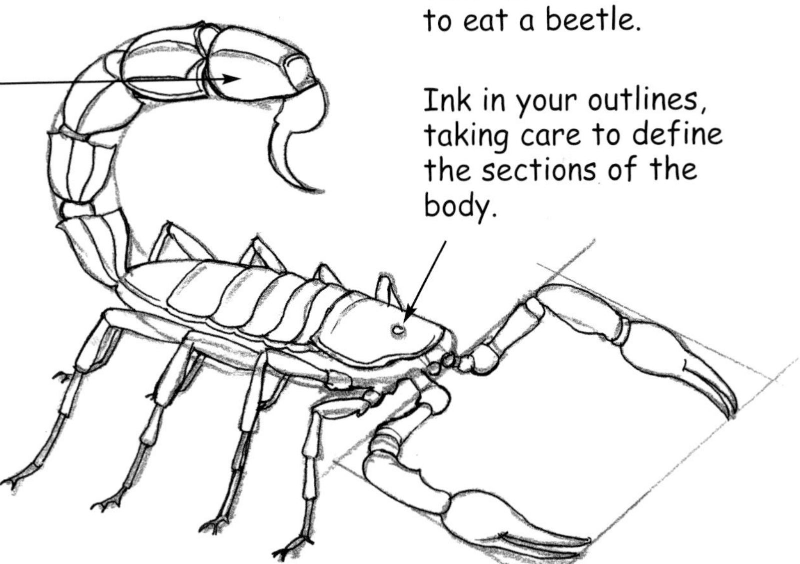

Scorpions are fierce killers, but good mothers. The female bears live young, rather than laying eggs. She carries her babies about with her on her back until they are ready to look after themselves.

Cockroach

The cockroach is a living fossil! One of Earth's oldest creatures, it has existed for 275 million years, hardly changing in that time. A true survival expert, it can live almost anywhere and eat almost anything. Some have adapted to live in human homes, and are major pests.

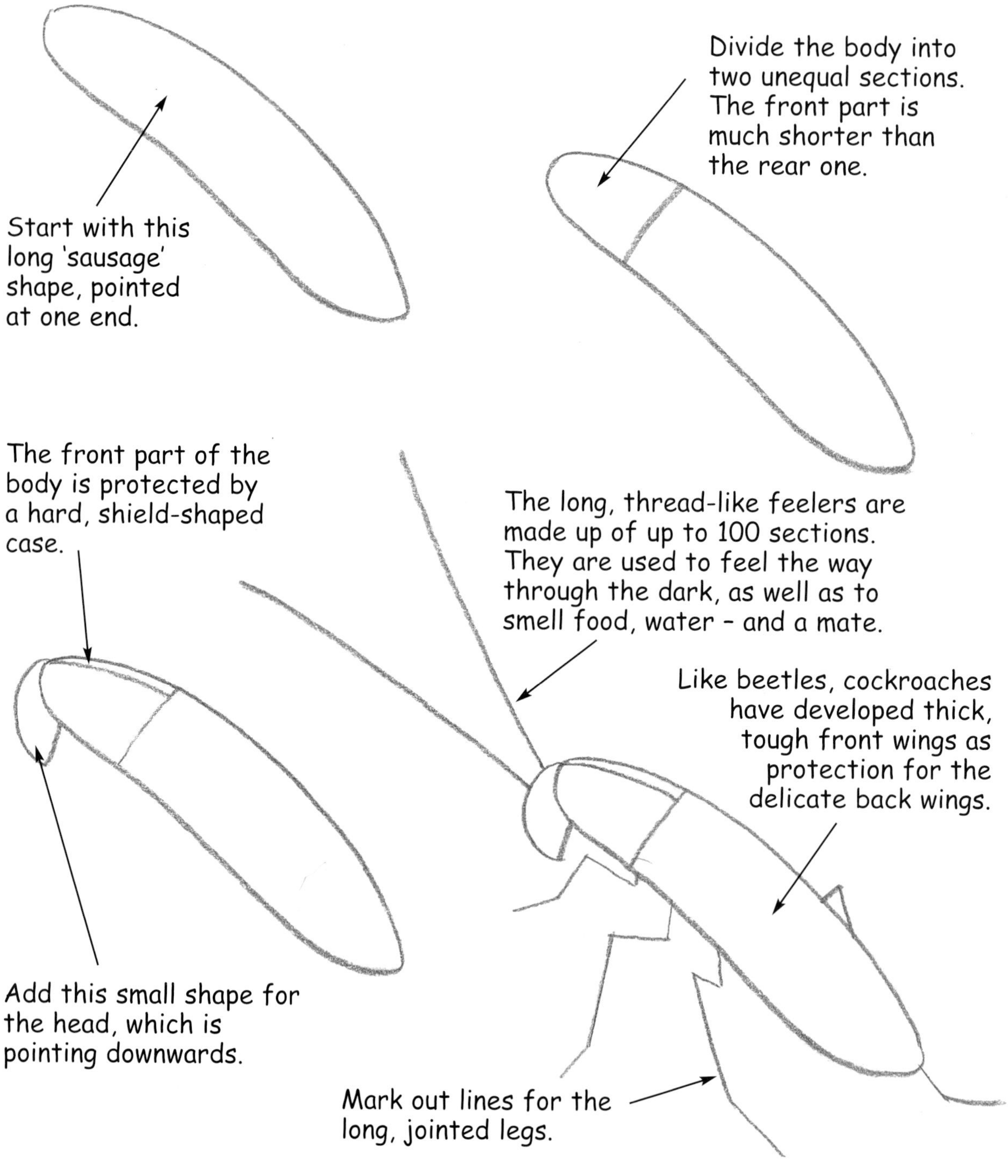
Start with this long 'sausage' shape, pointed at one end.
Divide the body into two unequal sections. The front part is much shorter than the rear one.
The front part of the body is protected by a hard, shield-shaped case.
Add this small shape for the head, which is pointing downwards.
The long, thread-like feelers are made up of up to 100 sections. They are used to feel the way through the dark, as well as to smell food, water – and a mate.
Like beetles, cockroaches have developed thick, tough front wings as protection for the delicate back wings.
Mark out lines for the long, jointed legs.

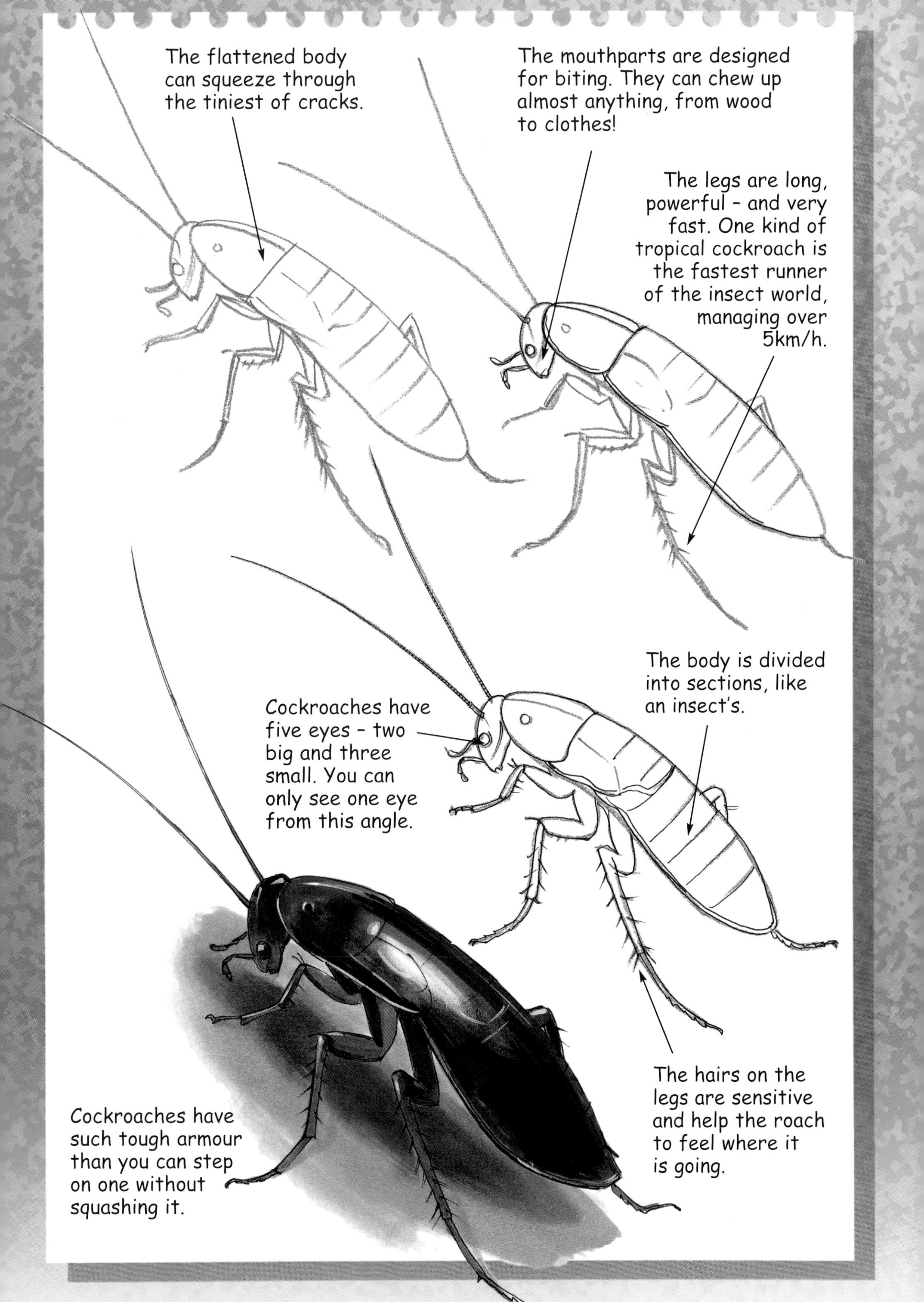

The flattened body can squeeze through the tiniest of cracks.
The mouthparts are designed for biting. They can chew up almost anything, from wood to clothes!
The legs are long, powerful – and very fast. One kind of tropical cockroach is the fastest runner of the insect world, managing over 5km/h.
The body is divided into sections, like an insect's.
Cockroaches have five eyes – two big and three small. You can only see one eye from this angle.
Cockroaches have such tough armour than you can step on one without squashing it.
The hairs on the legs are sensitive and help the roach to feel where it is going.

Ground Beetle

Ground beetles live up to their name: nearly all the 800 different kinds are grounded, with wings stuck permanently inside their cases. They are mostly active by night, when they run about looking for insects, slugs and snails to eat - so they are very helpful to farmers and gardeners.

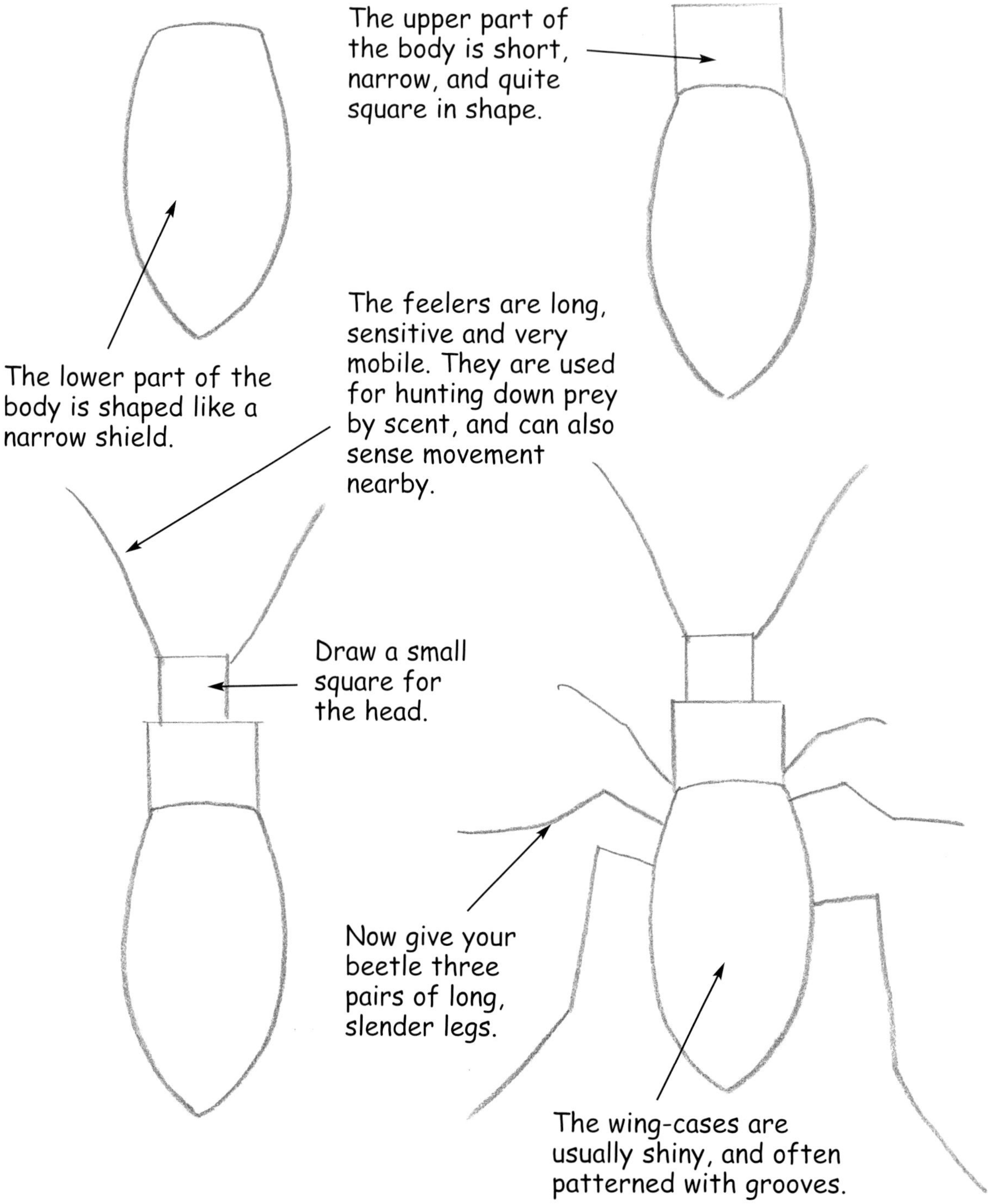

The lower part of the body is shaped like a narrow shield.
The upper part of the body is short, narrow, and quite square in shape.
The feelers are long, sensitive and very mobile. They are used for hunting down prey by scent, and can also sense movement nearby.
Draw a small square for the head.
Now give your beetle three pairs of long, slender legs.
The wing-cases are usually shiny, and often patterned with grooves.

The eyes are quite large. This insect has good vision.

The wing-cases are sealed together along their inner edges and cannot be opened.

Curve the edges of the top part of the body. This beetle has a 'square-shouldered' shape.

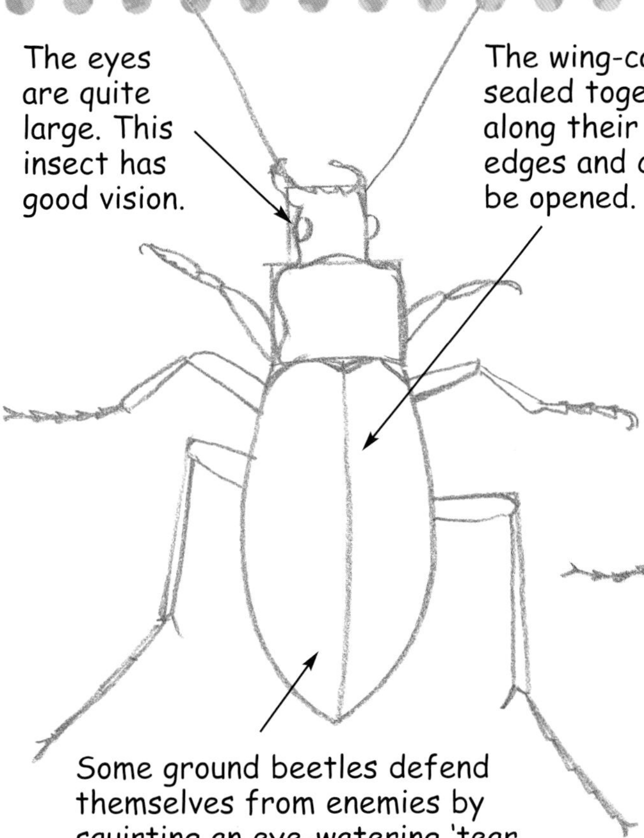

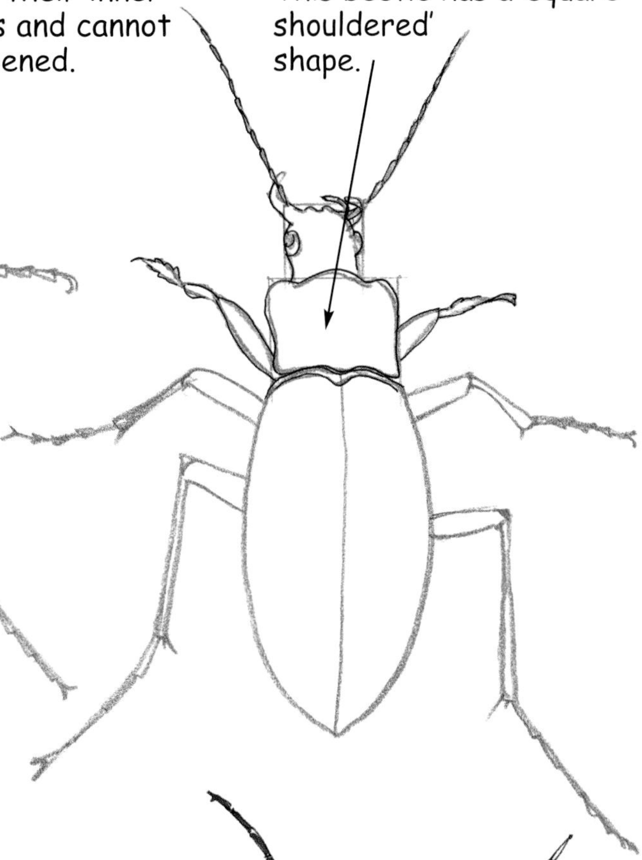

Some ground beetles defend themselves from enemies by squirting an eye-watering 'tear gas' from their rear ends.

Most ground beetles hide away under logs and stones by day and come out to hunt at night.

The end joints of the legs have five sections, and finish in two tiny claws.

Assassin Bug

We often use the word 'bug' for any creepy crawly. But when scientists talk about bugs they mean a special group of insects with beak-like mouths that stab and suck. This one gets its name of Assassin (murderer) from the speed with which it seizes and poisons its victims.

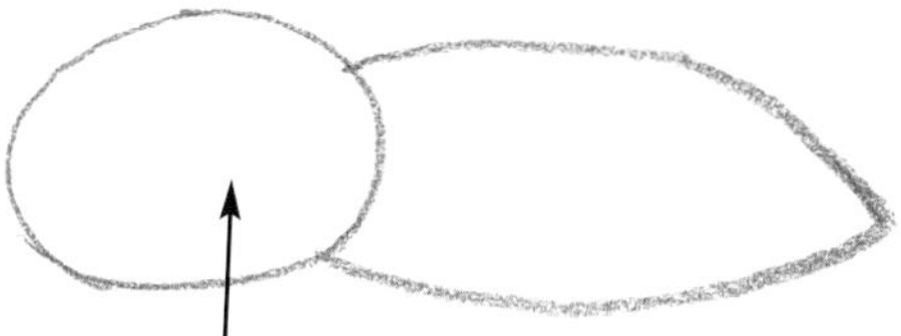

These two shapes form the body.

Add this shape for the narrow head, which looks too small for the body.

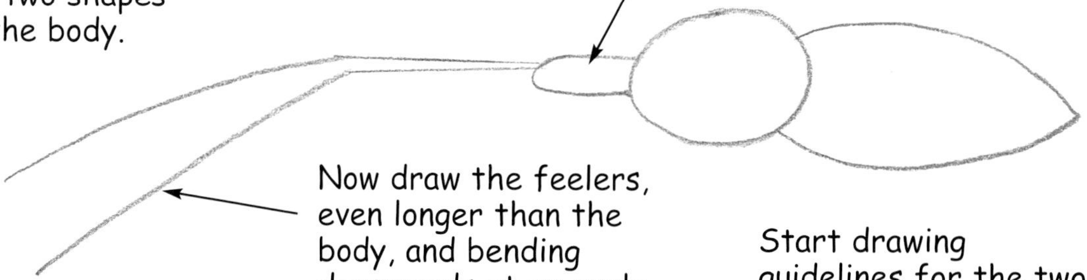

Now draw the feelers, even longer than the body, and bending downwards at an angle.

Start drawing guidelines for the two hind pairs of legs.

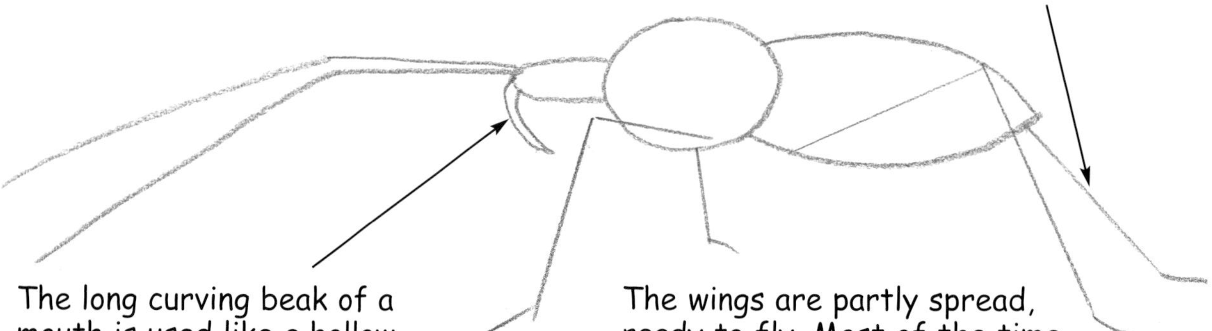

The long curving beak of a mouth is used like a hollow needle to stab into the victim's body. It squirts in poison to break down body tissues into a liquid, which it sucks up.

The wings are partly spread, ready to fly. Most of the time they are hidden inside wing-cases, like those of beetles.

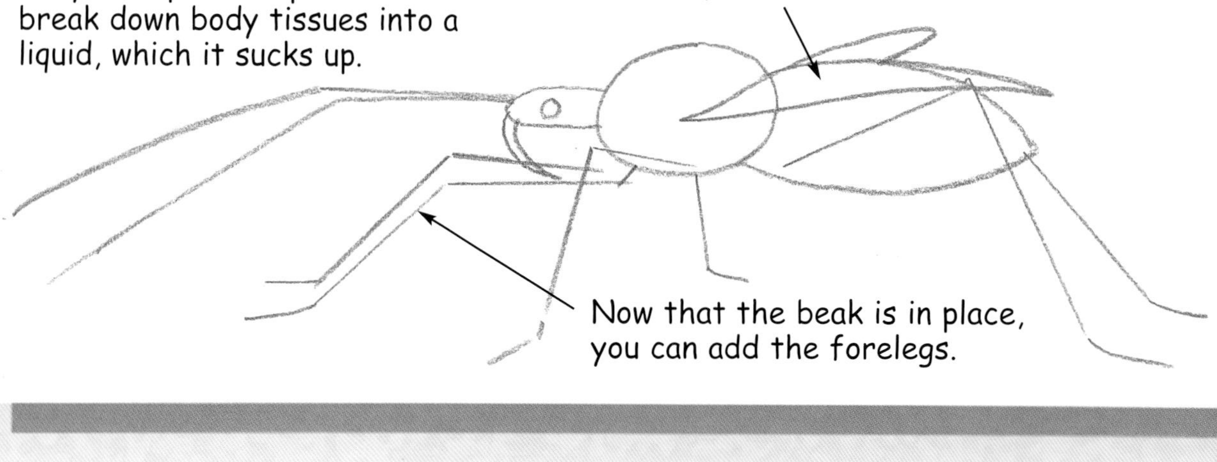

Now that the beak is in place, you can add the forelegs.

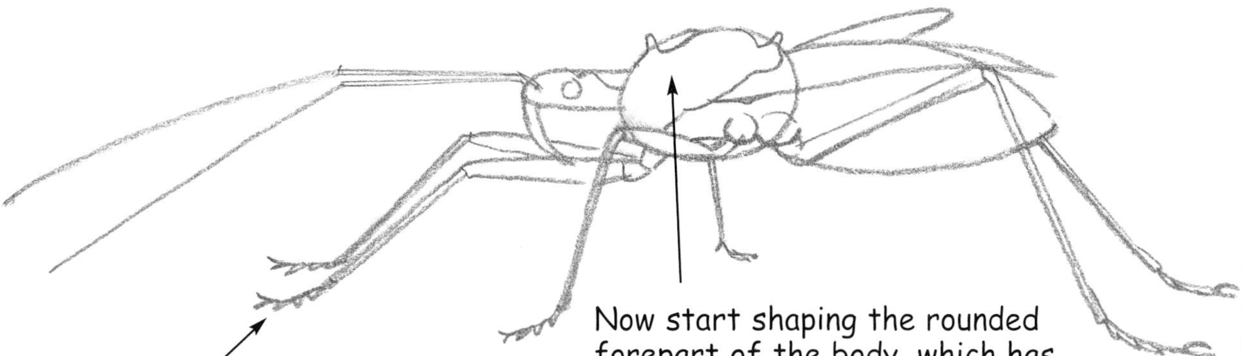

Now start shaping the rounded forepart of the body, which has two odd little 'shoulder-pad' knobs on its upper surface.

The powerful forelegs are used to grab prey. Some bugs lie in wait for their victims, others go out hunting and run down their prey.

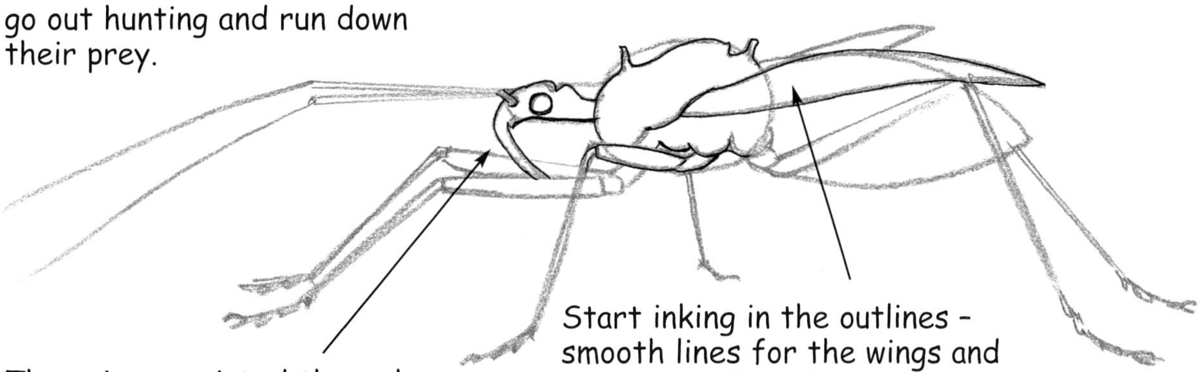

Start inking in the outlines – smooth lines for the wings and rear part of the body, more jagged ones for the knobbly front part.

The poison squirted through the mouthparts can kill an insect 400 times the Assassin's size in seconds.

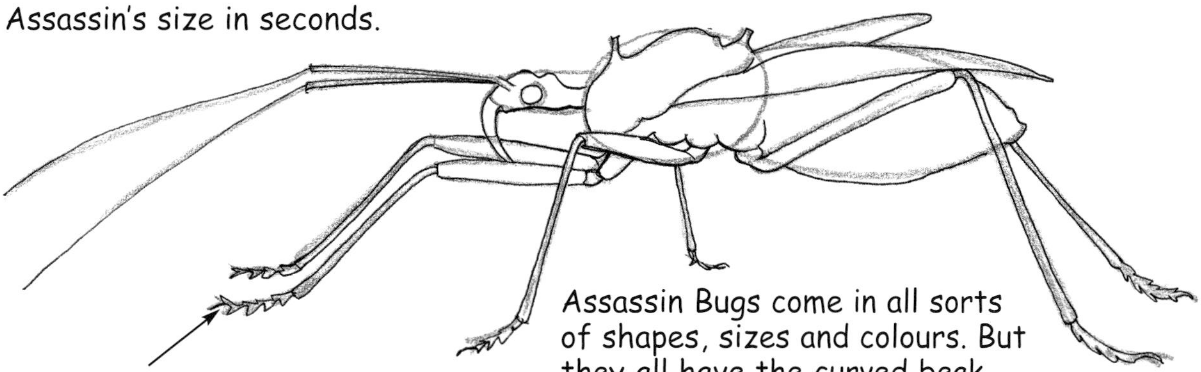

Assassin Bugs come in all sorts of shapes, sizes and colours. But they all have the curved beak and narrow head that gives them such a sinister look.

The feet end in sticky pads to give a better grip on prey.

Earwig

Earwigs like to crawl into small dark holes. They aren't particularly attracted to ears, but people feared they might be – and so they got their name. More suitable is their Latin name, which means 'little scissors', referring to the insect's pair of pincers.

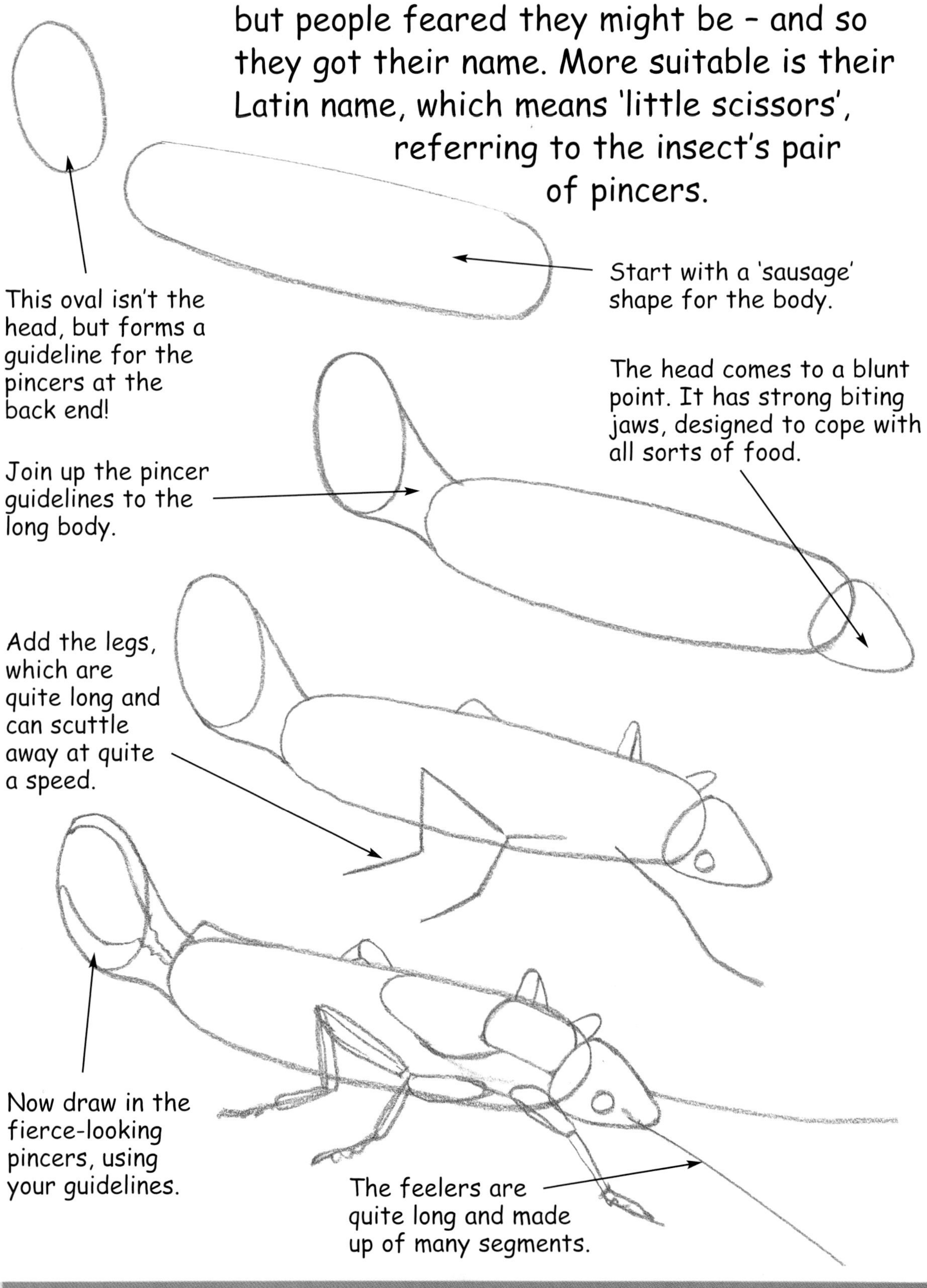

This oval isn't the head, but forms a guideline for the pincers at the back end!
Start with a 'sausage' shape for the body.
The head comes to a blunt point. It has strong biting jaws, designed to cope with all sorts of food.
Join up the pincer guidelines to the long body.
Add the legs, which are quite long and can scuttle away at quite a speed.
Now draw in the fierce-looking pincers, using your guidelines.
The feelers are quite long and made up of many segments.

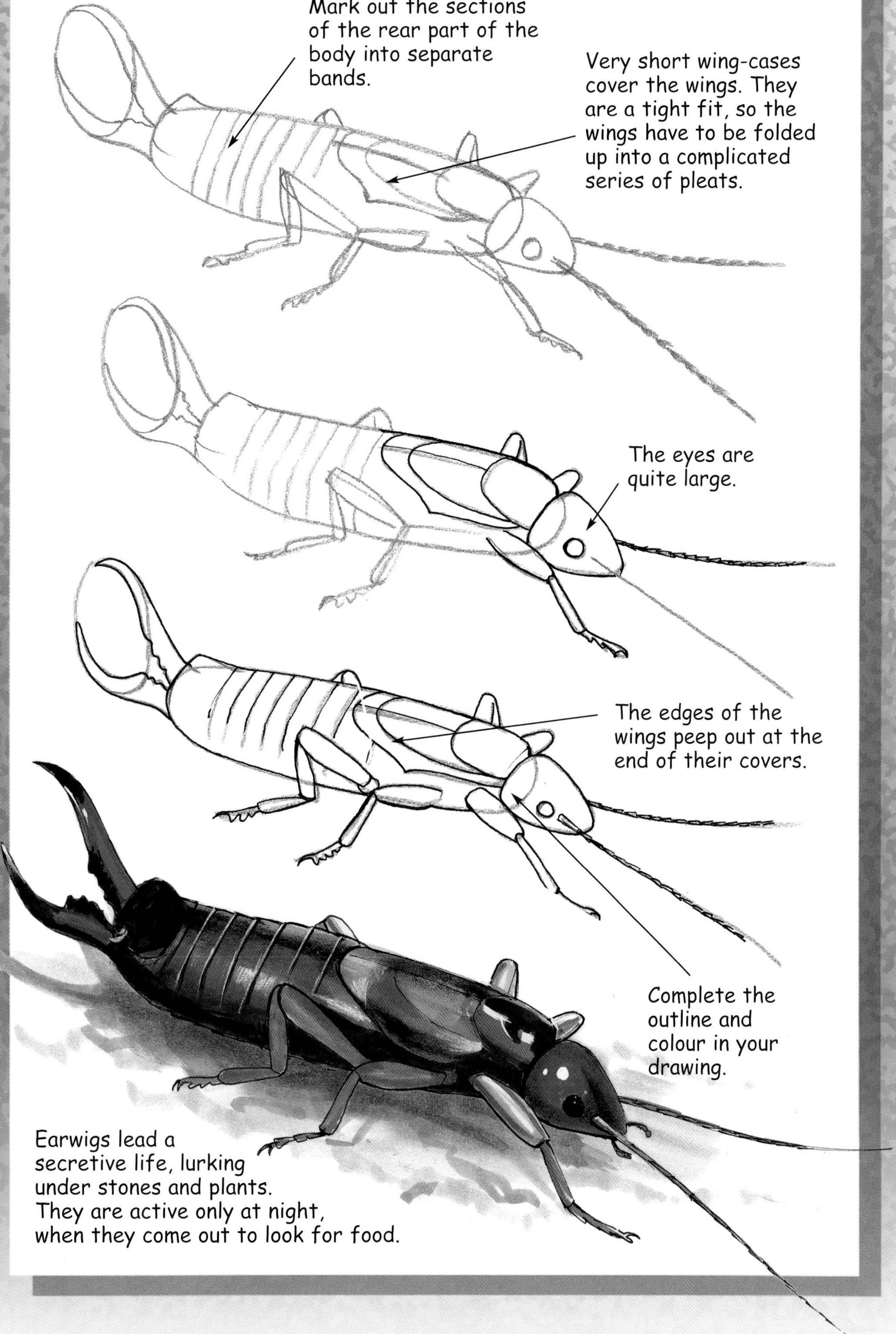
Mark out the sections of the rear part of the body into separate bands.
Very short wing-cases cover the wings. They are a tight fit, so the wings have to be folded up into a complicated series of pleats.
The eyes are quite large.
The edges of the wings peep out at the end of their covers.
Complete the outline and colour in your drawing.

Earwigs lead a secretive life, lurking under stones and plants. They are active only at night, when they come out to look for food.